A *Campbell* COOKBOOK

COOKING

WITH

SOUP

FIRST CANADIAN PRINTING, 1973 (ALSO AVAILABLE IN FRENCH). WRITE TO:
CAMPBELL SOUP COMPANY LTD, 60 BIRMINGHAM STREET, TORONTO, ONTARIO M8V 2B8

Table of Contents

Introduction . . .

Of all the convenience foods that give you a head start to better meals, soups are probably the most versatile.

When you open a can of soup—to use as soup, or as a sauce, or as a cooking ingredient—you have much of the work already done for you.

A casserole is half ready at the start when soup is the sauce—as are many other meat and vegetable dishes. Serve a bowl of soup and you have a meal well on the way. Just open a can of any of the following kinds for appealing eating and easier cooking.

Here are more than 40 kinds for your selection.

CONDENSED SOUPS

Asparagus, Cream of
Bean with Bacon
Beef with Vegetables and Barley
Beef Broth (Bouillon)
Beef Noodle
Celery, Cream of
Cheddar Cheese
Chicken, Cream of
Chicken Gumbo
Chicken Noodle
Chicken Noodle-O's
Chicken with Rice
Chicken & Stars
Chicken Vegetable
Clam Chowder Manhattan Style
Clam Chowder, New England
Consommé (Beef, getatin added)
French Canadian Style Pea
Golden Vegetable Noodle-O's
Green Pea
Minestrone

Mushroom, Cream of
Mushroom, Golden
Noodles & Ground Beef
Onion
Ox Tail
Oyster Stew
Potato, Cream of
Scotch Broth
Shrimp, Cream of
Tomato
Tomato Noodle-O's
Tomato, Bisque of
Tomato Rice, Old Fashioned
Turkey Noodle
Turkey Vegetable
Vegetable
Vegetable, Old Fashioned
Vegetable Beef
Vegetable, Cream of
Vegetarian,Vegetable

READY TO SERVE SOUPS

CHUNKY SOUPS

Beef
Chicken

Turkey
Vegetable

3

Meeting Nutritional Needs

Nutrition is what we eat and how our body uses it. It is what makes our bodies healthy and strong. It even affects our mental well being. Nutrition is not a "sometimes" thing. It is not one "good meal" a day. It is the total food and beverage consumed in a day, from morning until we retire at night. You are the decision-maker when it comes to what you eat yourself or serve to friends and family. You select it, purchase it, store it and prepare it. So it is important to know basic facts on nutrition as they relate to food consumption and meal planning. Don't forget to include food eaten away from home when planning your total daily intake.

Each of us has different nutritional needs, and these needs are constantly changing. Children's needs are dictated by their growth patterns. Adult needs change with age. One set of rules simply cannot apply to everyone. And, that is one of the reasons for much of the confusion today. Even the nutritional experts generalize by urging us to eat a "little bit of everything and not too much of any one thing". But what is "everything"? The following Food Guide is a basic answer.

DAILY FOOD GUIDE

WE SHOULD EAT EVERY DAY. (Note: Every Day)

Milk Group

Items in this group are a primary source of calcium. They also provide protein, riboflavin, and vitamin A.

2 to 3 cups of milk	— children under 9
3 or more cups	— children 9 to 12
4 or more cups	— teenagers
1½ to 2 cups	— adults
4 or more cups	— expectant and nursing mothers

This can be whole or skim milk, evaporated or dry milk, or buttermilk. 400 International Units of vitamin D are needed for all growing persons and expectant and nursing mothers.

Fruit-Vegetable Groups

Items in these groups are counted on to supply most of the ascorbic acid (vitamin C), as well as much of the vitamin A, some iron and other minerals.

2 servings of fruit or juice including a satisfactory source of vitamin C (ascorbic acid) such as oranges, tomatoes, or vitaminized apple juice.

1 serving of potatoes.

2 servings of other vegetables preferably yellow or leafy green and often raw.

Meat and Fish Group

Items in this group supply protein, iron, thiamine, riboflavin, and niacin.

1 serving of meat, fish, or poultry.

Eat liver occasionally.

Eggs and cheese may be used in place of meat; and in addition each should be served at least three times a week.

Dried beans or peas also contribute to this group.

Bread-Cereal Group

Items in this group supply many of the vitamins in the B group, iron, calcium, and carbohydrate.

4 servings or more of enriched or whole-grain breads and cereals. This group also includes enriched flour, macaroni and spaghetti, noodles, rice and rolled oats, etc.

One serving is 1 slice of bread, 1 ounce ready-to-eat cereal, ½ to ¾ cup cooked cereal, cornmeal, macaroni, rice, noodles, or spaghetti.

To round out meals, experts urge us to include foods not included within the Groups. These might include butter, margarine, sugars . . . many of which are often found in everyday meal patterns or as ingredients in recipes. Some vegetable oil can also be included among the fats used.

For soups that contribute to the Daily Food Guide see page 130.

*"To make the best,
begin with the best—
then cook with extra care."*

Easy Rules for Cooking with Condensed Soups

A can of condensed soup is a constant help in your kitchen—whether you use it for white sauce in a casserole or for cooking liquid in a stew.

The cream soups, which are useful in so many recipes, include:

Cream of Celery	Cream of Mushroom
Cream of Chicken	

Often one kind of cream soup may be substituted for another. You will find recipes suggesting this all through the book.

Other soups with countless uses are:

Cheddar Cheese	Golden Mushroom	Tomato

The following chart gives you some "rules of thumb" to use in creating your own recipes with condensed soups as cooking sauces (see SAUCERY chapter for special sauces with specific directions):

Tomato Souper Sauce	Use condensed tomato soup just as it comes from the can or thin a bit with water, if desired. Season as you like with a little prepared mustard, horse-radish, herbs, Worcestershire, etc. Use as pour-on sauce for hamburgers, pork chops, and other meats.
Gravy	Add a can of condensed cream soup or golden mush-room soup to 2 to 3 tablespoons of meat drippings (or butter); stir in ¼ cup of water or more for thickness desired.

White Sauce or Cream Sauce	Use canned condensed cream soups or Cheddar cheese soup in almost any recipe that calls for white sauce or cream sauce. Thin with ¼ to ½ cup milk or water for medium white sauce for dishes such as creamed chicken or creamed vegetables. One can makes enough sauce for ½ to 1 cup diced or chopped cooked meat (chicken, turkey, ham, tuna, shrimp, crab) or 4 sliced hardcooked eggs . . . plus seasonings as desired.
	One can soup also makes enough pour-on sauce for: 1 pound meat as meat loaf, 1 pound fish fillets, 2 pounds chicken parts, 2 cups cooked vegetables (two 15 fluid ounce cans; two 10-12 ounce packages, frozen), 6 chops, 4 to 6 sandwiches.
Casseroles	1 can of any condensed cream soup (or Cheddar cheese or tomato soup) plus ¼ cup water or milk (or more as needed) makes enough sauce for about 2 cups cooked macaroni or noodles (about 4 ounces uncooked) or 1½ cups cooked rice (about ½ cup uncooked). Add seasonings and cooked meat or vegetables as desired.
Meat Stock or Broth	Use canned condensed beef broth or consommé in place of homemade stock. Good for many kinds of stews and pot roasts.
Chicken Stew	Use any of the cream soups, or chicken soups for part of water for cooking. If using a vegetable soup or one with noodles or rice, add towards end of cooking time.
Meat Stew or Pot Roast	Use consommé, beef broth, golden mushroom or tomato soup for part of liquid to cook meat. For vegetables in stew, use one of vegetable soups; add towards end of cooking time since vegetables are already cooked.
Homemade Soup	Add canned condensed soup for flavour and body.

Note about using this book: Asterisks (*) are used in menus to show items for which there are recipes. Recipes are listed in index at end of book.

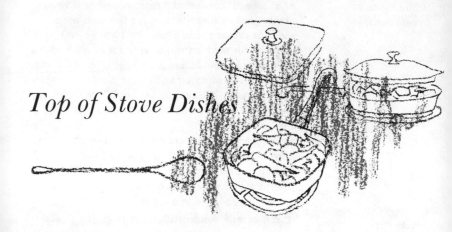

Top of Stove Dishes

A delicious dish you cook in one pan—and quickly. Who could ask more? No wonder homemakers grow enthusiastic about the flavour, ease, and wonderful versatility of these favourite main dishes.

The basics of frying pan cooking are simple. Have a heavy-bottom pan that heats evenly, roomy enough to hold all the ingredients without crowding. (Of course, many of the recipes may be prepared in a chafing dish, large heavy saucepan, or one of the electric utensils.)

Combine foods. As in casseroles, most of these recipes call for meat or fish or cheese—plus a pasta or potatoes—plus sauce. Condensed soups used as sauces give luscious flavour, mingling through all the ingredients and resulting in irresistible eating. See how often the recipes suggest using one soup for another to give a slight flavour variation—as you prefer.

Serve your quick supper dish piping hot, with a crisp salad and warm rolls. Now—collect the compliments.

SEAFOOD MARYLAND

1 can (10 fl. ounces) condensed cream of mushroom soup
½ cup light cream
2 cups diced cooked seafood (lobster, shrimp, white fish)
1 tablespoon chopped parsley
1 teaspoon lemon juice
Toast

In saucepan, combine all ingredients except toast. Heat; stir now and then. Serve over toast. 4 to 6 servings.

MACARONI AND CHEESE

¼ cup chopped onion
1 tablespoon butter or margarine
1 can (10 fl. ounces) condensed
  Cheddar cheese soup
½ cup milk
3 cups cooked macaroni

Cook onion in butter until tender. Blend in soup; gradually add milk. Heat; stir often. Mix in macaroni. Heat, stirring. 4 to 6 servings.

BEEF MEXICALI

1 boneless chuck (about 3 ½
  pounds)
2 tablespoons flour
2 tablespoons shortening
1 can (14 fl. ounces) tomatoes
½ cup water
1 cup chopped onion
½ cup diced green pepper
1 tablespoon chili powder
1 can (10 fl. ounces) condensed
  beef with vegetables and barley
  soup
Corn bread or cooked rice

Cut meat into thin strips, trim fat; sprinkle with flour. In frying pan, brown meat in shortening; pour off fat. Add remaining ingredients except soup and corn bread. Cover; cook over low heat 1 hour. Stir now and then. Add soup; cook covered ½ hour longer or until tender. Stir now and then. Serve over corn bread or cooked rice. 6 servings.

YUMMY PORCUPINE MEATBALLS

1 can (10 fl. ounces) condensed
  tomato soup
1 pound ground beef
1 cup cooked rice
1 egg, slightly beaten
¼ cup finely chopped onion
1 teaspoon salt
1 small clove garlic, minced
2 tablespoons shortening
½ soup can water
1 teaspoon prepared mustard

Mix ¼ cup soup with beef, rice, egg, onion, and salt. Shape firmly into 16 meatballs. Brown meatballs and garlic in shortening; pour off fat. Blend in remaining soup, water, and mustard. Cover; simmer for 20 minutes or until done. Stir now and then. 4 servings.

9

CHICKEN HASH

1 can (10 fl. ounces) condensed
    cream of mushroom soup
⅓ to ½ cup milk
1 can (6 ounces) boned chicken or
    turkey, or 1 cup diced cooked
    chicken or turkey
1 cup cooked cut green beans
2 tablespoons diced pimiento
Dash nutmeg
Dash pepper
3 cups hot cooked rice

Blend soup and milk; add chicken, beans, pimiento, nutmeg, and pepper. Heat slowly; stir often. Serve over cooked rice. 3 to 4 servings.

SOUPER LEFTOVERS

Leftover roast, steak, or chicken,
    chopped (about 1 cup)
Leftover vegetables (about ½ cup)
1 can (10 fl. ounces) condensed
    cream of celery soup
Milk or water as needed
Crisp toast slices

Combine all ingredients except toast. Heat and serve on toast or in hot patty shells—a tasty way to "make a meal" out of small amounts of meat and vegetables.
VARIATIONS: Substitute cream of chicken, mushroom, or tomato soup for cream of celery soup.

HE-MAN SPANISH RICE

1 pound ground beef
½ cup chopped green pepper
½ cup chopped onion
1 large clove garlic, minced
1 can (10 fl. ounces) condensed
    tomato soup
1½ cups water
1½ cups quick-cooking rice,
    uncooked
1 tablespoon Worcestershire
½ teaspoon salt
Generous dash pepper

In frying pan, cook beef, green pepper, and onion with garlic until vegetables are tender; stir to separate meat. Add remaining ingredients. Cover; cook over low heat 10 minutes or until liquid is absorbed. 4 servings.

VEAL PARMESAN

1 pound thin veal cutlet
1 egg, beaten
½ cup bread crumbs
2 tablespoons shortening
1 can (10 fl. ounces) condensed
    tomato soup
½ soup can water
¼ cup minced onion
1 clove garlic, minced
Dash thyme
4 ounces Mozzarella cheese, thinly
    sliced
Grated Parmesan cheese

Dip veal cutlet in egg, then in bread crumbs. Brown in shortening in oven-proof pan. Add soup, water, onion, garlic, and thyme. Cook over low heat 45 minutes or until tender; stir now and then. Top with Mozzarella cheese; sprinkle with grated Parmesan cheese. Broil until cheese melts. 4 servings.

WIENERS 'N NOODLES

1 pound wieners, cut in half
    diagonally
½ cup chopped onion
½ teaspoon basil or oregano
    leaves, crushed
2 tablespoons butter or margarine
1 can (10 fl. ounces) condensed
    cream of celery or mushroom soup
½ cup milk
½ cup chopped canned tomatoes
2 cups cooked wide noodles
2 tablespoons chopped parsley

In frying pan, brown wieners and cook onion with basil in butter until tender. Stir in remaining ingredients. Heat; stir now and then. 4 servings.

CHOP SOUPY

1 pound round steak, cut in very
    thin strips
2 tablespoons salad oil
1 can (10 fl. ounces) condensed
    golden mushroom soup
½ cup water
1 tablespoon soy sauce
1½ cups diagonally sliced celery
1 cup green pepper cut in 1-inch
    squares
½ cup green onion diagonally cut
    in 1-inch pieces
Cooked rice

In frying pan, brown beef in oil. Add remaining ingredients except rice. Cover; cook over low heat 20 minutes or until meat is tender. Stir now and then. Serve over rice. 4 servings.

SPAGHETTI SOUTHERN STYLE

2 slices bacon
1 cup diced cooked beef
1 medium green pepper, sliced
1 medium onion, sliced
¼ to ½ teaspoon chili powder
1 clove garlic, minced
1 can (10 fl. ounces) condensed tomato soup
½ soup can water
7 ounces spaghetti, cooked

Cook bacon in frying pan until crisp; remove and crumble. In drippings, cook beef, pepper, onion, chili powder, and garlic until vegetables are tender. Add soup, water, and bacon. Cover; cook over low heat 30 minutes. Stir often. Serve over hot spaghetti. 3 to 4 servings.

SPAGHETTI WIENER SUPPER

½ cup chopped celery
½ cup chopped onion
2 tablespoons shortening
1 pound wieners, cut in ½-inch slices
1 can (10 fl. ounces) condensed tomato soup
½ cup water
1 teaspoon Worcestershire
7 ounces spaghetti, cooked

Cook celery and onion in shortening until tender. Add wieners; cook until lightly browned. Stir in soup, water, and Worcestershire. Cook about 15 minutes to blend flavours; stir often. Serve over hot cooked spaghetti. 3 to 4 servings.

TUNA SHORTCAKE

1 can (10 fl. ounces) condensed cream of celery, chicken, or mushroom soup
½ cup milk
1 can (7 ounces) tuna, drained and flaked
1 cup cooked peas
1 tablespoon chopped pimiento
Hot biscuits or toast

Blend soup and milk; add tuna, peas, and pimiento. Heat; stir often. Serve over biscuits or toast. 3 to 4 servings.

SKILLET CHICKEN DELIGHT

2 pounds chicken parts
¼ cup flour
¼ cup butter or margarine
1 can (10 fl. ounces) condensed chicken gumbo soup
½ soup can water
2 tablespoons ketchup

Dust chicken with flour; brown in butter. Stir in soup, water, and ketchup. Cover; simmer 45 minutes or until chicken is tender. Stir often. 4 to 6 servings.

TUNA À LA KING

½ cup sliced celery
2 tablespoons chopped onion
1 tablespoon butter or margarine
1 can (10 fl. ounces) condensed
  cream of mushroom soup
½ cup milk
1 can (7 ounces) tuna, drained
  and flaked
2 tablespoons chopped pimiento
Chopped parsley
4 slices toast

In saucepan, cook celery and onion in butter until tender. Blend in soup; gradually stir in milk. Add tuna and pimiento. Heat; stir now and then. Garnish with parsley. Serve over toast. 4 servings.

LAST MINUTE SUPPER

1 can (12 ounces) luncheon meat,
  cut in strips
1 medium onion, thinly sliced
2 tablespoons butter or margarine
1 can (10 fl. ounces) condensed
  cream of mushroom soup
½ cup milk
2 cups cubed cooked potatoes
  (about 4 medium)
2 tablespoons chopped parsley
Dash pepper

Lightly brown meat and onion in butter until onion is tender. Blend in soup and milk. Add remaining ingredients; cook over low heat 10 minutes or until flavours are blended. Stir often. 4 servings.

TUNA BEAN SUPPER DISH

⅓ cup chopped onion
2 tablespoons butter or margarine
1 can (10 fl. ounces) condensed
  beef broth
1⅓ cups quick-cooking rice,
  uncooked
¼ cup sliced water chestnuts
1 teaspoon soy sauce
2 cans (about 7 ounces each) tuna,
  drained and flaked
1 cup cooked green beans

In saucepan, cook onion in butter until tender. Add broth, rice, water chestnuts, and soy. Bring to a vigorous boil. Cover; cook over low heat about 5 minutes or until all liquid is absorbed. Add tuna and beans; heat. Serve with additional soy. 4 servings.

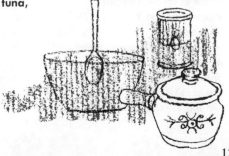

Casseroles to Your Credit

Hail to the casserole, favourite way to bring a tasty meal to the table, right in its baking dish.

Choose your own reason for making a casserole tonight. You probably have the ingredients on hand—some meat or fish or poultry—plus a pasta or rice or potatoes to extend them? Add a vegetable for contrast in texture and colour.

Now for the perfect sauce that's ready at your fingertips—select a can of soup. It will season and blend together all the other ingredients. The cream soups—cream of celery, mushroom, chicken, and Cheddar cheese —go perfectly in almost any combination. Tomato soup also wins honours as a sauce. Often you'll find that one soup can be substituted for another in these recipes. Stir in the soup and your casserole is ready to bake.

Casseroles can be prepared in advance, refrigerated (or often frozen) and baked before serving (allow extra baking time). There's no worry about delay—a casserole waits in a low oven. If the children are to eat ahead, just prepare several smaller baking dishes, or individual servings.

Unexpected company coming? Reach for a can of soup, spaghetti, a can of tuna . . . another good casserole is on the way.

PERFECT TUNA

1 can (10 fl. ounces) condensed cream of celery, chicken, or mushroom soup
¼ cup milk
1 can (7 ounces) tuna, drained and flaked
2 hard-cooked eggs, sliced
1 cup cooked peas
1 cup slightly crumbled potato chips

In 1-quart casserole, blend soup and milk; stir in tuna, eggs, and peas. Top with chips. Bake in a 350° oven 30 minutes. 3 to 4 servings.

TOMATO BEEF CASSEROLE

1 medium onion, chopped
1 tablespoon shortening
1 can (10 fl. ounces) condensed
  tomato soup
½ cup water
1 cup cubed cooked beef
½ cup cooked cut green beans
1 cup cooked noodles
½ cup shredded Canadian
  Cheddar cheese

Lightly brown onion in shortening. Add remaining ingredients except cheese. Pour into a 1-quart casserole. Top with cheese. Bake in a 375° oven 25 minutes or until hot and bubbly. 4 servings.

VARIATION: If desired, ½ pound ground beef can be browned with the onion and substituted for the cooked beef.

WIENER NOODLE BAKE

8 wieners, sliced
¼ cup chopped onion
2 tablespoons butter or margarine
2 cups cooked medium noodles
1 can (10 fl. ounces) condensed
  tomato soup
½ cup water
1 teaspoon prepared mustard
¼ cup buttered bread crumbs

Brown wieners and cook onion in butter until tender. Combine with noodles, soup, water, and mustard in 1½-quart casserole; top with crumbs. Bake in a 350° oven 30 minutes. 4 servings.

CHICKEN PIE

1½ cups cubed cooked chicken
1 cup cubed cooked potatoes
1 cup cooked mixed vegetables
1 can (10 fl. ounces) condensed
  cream of chicken soup
½ cup milk
1 tablespoon finely chopped onion
Generous dash poultry seasoning
1 cup biscuit mix
¼ cup cold water

In 1½-quart casserole, combine all ingredients except biscuit mix and water. Bake at 450°F. for 15 minutes; stir. Meanwhile, combine biscuit mix and water as directed on package; spoon 6 biscuits around edge of casserole. Bake 15 minutes more or until biscuits are done. 4 servings.

SAVOURY SPAGHETTI CASSEROLE

1 pound ground beef
½ cup chopped onion
¼ cup chopped green pepper
2 tablespoons butter or margarine
1 can (10 fl. ounces) condensed
    cream of mushroom soup
1 can (10 fl. ounces) condensed
    tomato soup
1 soup can water
1 clove garlic, minced
1 cup shredded sharp process
    cheese
½ pound spaghetti, cooked and
    drained

Cook beef, onion, and green pepper in butter until meat is lightly browned and vegetables are tender; stir to separate meat particles. Add soups, water, and garlic; heat. Blend with ½ cup cheese and cooked spaghetti in a 3-quart casserole; top with remaining cheese. Bake in a 350° oven 30 minutes or until bubbling and hot. 4 to 6 servings.

TURKEY STROGANOFF

¼ cup chopped green pepper
2 tablespoons chopped onion
2 tablespoons butter or margarine
1 can (10 fl. ounces) condensed
    cream of mushroom soup
½ cup sour cream
¼ cup milk
2 cups cooked noodles
1½ cups diced cooked turkey
½ teaspoon paprika

Cook green pepper and onion in butter until tender. In 1-quart casserole, blend soup, sour cream and milk; stir in remaining ingredients. Bake in a 350° oven 35 minutes. 4 servings.

SEAFOOD POTATO PIE

½ cup sliced celery
2 tablespoons chopped onion
2 tablespoons butter or margarine
1 can (10 fl. ounces) condensed
    cream of mushroom soup
½ cup milk
1½ cups diced cooked shrimp
1 cup cooked peas
Dash ground thyme
2 cups mashed potatoes
¼ cup shredded process cheese

In saucepan, cook celery and onion in butter until tender. Blend in soup, milk, shrimp, peas, and thyme. Pour into 1½-quart casserole. Bake at 350° F. for 25 minutes; stir. Arrange potatoes around edge of casserole; sprinkle with cheese. Bake 5 minutes more. 4 servings.

FIX AHEAD CHICKEN

2 pounds chicken parts
2 tablespoons shortening
1 can (10 fl. ounces) condensed
   cream of chicken soup
½ soup can milk
¼ teaspoon poultry seasoning
¼ teaspoon salt
Dash pepper
4 medium carrots, cut lengthwise
   in quarters
6 small onions
1 package (10 ounces) frozen lima
   beans

Brown chicken in shortening; place in a 2-quart casserole. Discard drippings. Stir soup, milk, and seasonings together; heat. Add carrots and onions. Cover; cook over low heat for 10 minutes; stir often. Add lima beans; cook until separated; stir often. Pour over chicken. Cover; immediately refrigerate until 1 hour and 15 minutes before serving. Bake, covered, in a 375° oven for 1 hour. Uncover; bake 15 minutes more or until chicken is tender. If cooked for serving immediately (not refrigerated) decrease baking time of covered casserole 15 minutes. 4 generous servings.

TUNA OR CHICKEN CASSEROLE

1 can (10 fl. ounces) condensed
   cream of celery soup
½ cup milk
2 cups cooked noodles
1 can (7 ounces) tuna, drained and
   flaked
2 tablespoons diced pimiento
2 tablespoons chopped parsley
2 tablespoons buttered bread
   crumbs

Blend soup and milk. Add noodles, tuna, pimiento, and parsley. Pour into 1½-quart casserole; top with crumbs. Bake in a 350° oven for 30 minutes or until hot and bubbling. 3 to 4 servings. VARIATIONS: Substitute 1 can (6 ounces) boned chicken for tuna. Use Cheddar cheese, cream of mushroom, or chicken soup in place of cream of celery soup.

SPINACH MUSHROOM CASSEROLE

2 packages (12 ounces each)
   frozen spinach, cooked and
   drained
2 cups cooked noodles
1 cup shredded process cheese
1 can (10 fl. ounces) condensed
   cream of mushroom soup
½ cup milk
⅛ teaspoon ground nutmeg

Arrange layers of spinach, noodles, and ¾ cup cheese in 1½-quart baking dish or casserole. Blend soup with milk and nutmeg; pour over. Top with remaining cheese. Bake in 350° oven 30 minutes. 4 servings.

FAVOURITE HAM 'N POTATO BAKE

1 can (10 fl. ounces) condensed
   cream of celery, chicken, or
   mushroom soup
½ to ¾ cup milk
Dash pepper
4 cups sliced potatoes
1 cup diced cooked ham
1 small onion, sliced
1 tablespoon butter or margarine
Paprika

Combine soup, milk, and pepper. In buttered 2-quart casserole, arrange layers of potatoes, ham, onion, and soup sauce. (Be sure ham is covered to prevent drying.) Dot top with butter; sprinkle with paprika. Cover. Bake in a 375° oven for 1 hour. Uncover; bake 15 minutes or until potatoes are done. 4 servings. VARIATION: Substitute 1 cup diced cooked chicken for ham.

MACARONI AND CHEESE—FAMILY STYLE

½ cup ground or finely chopped
   cooked ham
¼ cup chopped onion
2 tablespoons butter or margarine
1 can (10 fl. ounces) condensed
   cream of mushroom soup
½ cup water
1½ cups shredded sharp Canadian
   Cheddar cheese
3 cups cooked macaroni
2 tablespoons buttered bread
   crumbs

Lightly brown ham and onion in butter. Stir in soup, milk, and 1 cup cheese. Heat until cheese melts; stir often. Blend sauce with macaroni; pour into buttered 1½-quart casserole. Sprinkle remaining cheese and crumbs on top. Bake in a 350° oven 30 minutes or until nicely browned and bubbling. Makes 4 servings.

OYSTER 'N HAM NOODLE BAKE

1 cup chopped cooked ham
1/4 cup chopped onion
2 tablespoons butter or margarine
2 tablespoons flour
1 can (10 fl. ounces) condensed
  oyster stew
1/4 cup milk
Dash hot pepper sauce
1 1/2 cups cooked noodles
Grated Parmesan cheese

In saucepan, brown ham and cook onion in butter until tender. Blend in flour; gradually stir in stew, milk, and hot pepper sauce. Cook, stirring until thickened. In 1-quart casserole, combine soup mixture with noodles. Top with cheese. Bake at 350°F. for 30 minutes or until hot. 4 servings.

PORK CHOP-BEAN BAKE

6 pork chops (about 1 1/2 pounds)
1 can (10 fl. ounces) condensed
  cream of celery or mushroom
  soup
2 packages (10 ounces each) cut
  green beans, cooked and drained
Dash crushed thyme leaves
1/4 teaspoon salt
1/8 teaspoon pepper

In oven-proof pan, brown chops; remove from pan. Pour off fat; stir in soup, beans, and thyme. Arrange chops on top; sprinkle with salt and pepper. Cover; bake at 350°F. for 1 hour or until chops are tender. 4 servings.

BUBBLING FISH BAKE

1/4 cup chopped onion
2 tablespoons butter or margarine
1 can (10 fl. ounces) condensed
  cream of celery, or mushroom
  soup
1/2 cup milk
1 cup shredded sharp Canadian
  Cheddar cheese
2 cups cooked macaroni or noodles
1 can (7 3/4 ounces) salmon, or 1
  can (7 ounces) tuna, drained
  and flaked
2 tablespoons buttered bread
  crumbs

Cook onion in butter until tender. Stir in soup, milk, 3/4 cup cheese, macaroni, and fish. Pour into a 1 1/2-quart casserole. Top with bread crumbs and remaining cheese. Bake in a 350° oven 30 minutes or until lightly browned and bubbling. 4 servings.

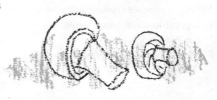

CHICK 'N HAM BAKE

½ cup canned sliced mushrooms, drained
2 tablespoons chopped onion
2 tablespoons chopped green pepper
1 small clove garlic, minced
Dash leaf thyme
2 tablespoons butter or margarine
1 can (10 fl. ounces) condensed cream of chicken soup
2 cups cooked spaghetti
1 ½ cups diced cooked ham
1 cup cooked tomatoes

Cook mushrooms, onion, green pepper, garlic, and thyme in butter until tender. Combine with remaining ingredients; pour into buttered 1½-quart casserole. Bake in a 350° oven 30 minutes. 4 servings.

OVEN MACARONI

¼ cup chopped onion
1 tablespoon butter or margarine
1 can (10 fl. ounces) condensed Cheddar cheese soup
½ cup milk
3 cups cooked macaroni
2 tablespoons buttered bread crumbs

Cook onion in butter until tender. Blend in soup; gradually stir in milk. In 1½-quart casserole, combine sauce and cooked macaroni. Sprinkle crumbs on top. Bake in a 350° oven about 30 minutes or until browned and bubbling. 4 servings.

PINWHEEL CASSEROLE

1 ½ cups cubed cooked beef, lamb, pork, or veal
¼ teaspoon oregano, crushed
2 tablespoons butter or margarine
1 can (10 fl. ounces) condensed golden mushroom soup
½ cup water
½ cup chopped canned tomatoes
1 cup cooked cut green beans
1 cup biscuit mix
2 tablespoons grated Parmesan cheese

In saucepan, brown meat with oregano in butter. Stir in soup, ¼ cup water, tomatoes, and green beans. Pour into 1½-quart casserole. Bake at 450°F. for 10 minutes. Meanwhile, combine biscuit mix and ¼ cup cold water; mix as directed on package. Roll out into 8-inch square; sprinkle with cheese. Roll up jelly roll fashion; cut into 8 slices. Place biscuits around edge. Bake 15 minutes more or until browned. 4 servings.

SHRIMP 'N SHELL CASSEROLE

1 can (10 fl. ounces) condensed
　cream of celery soup
¼ cup milk
1 tablespoon sherry
½ teaspoon curry powder
1 ½ cups diced cooked shrimp
2 cups cooked shell macaroni
2 tablespoons chopped parsley

In 1-quart casserole, blend soup, milk, sherry, and curry powder. Add remaining ingredients. Bake at 350°F. for 30 minutes; stir. 4 servings.

WIENER-POTATO BAKE

¼ cup chopped onion
1 tablespoon butter or margarine
1 can (10 fl. ounces) condensed
　cream of celery soup
½ cup milk
1 tablespoon prepared mustard
4 cups sliced cooked potatoes
　(about 4 medium)
6 wieners, slashed

In saucepan, cook onion in butter until tender; stir in soup, milk, and mustard. In shallow baking dish (10x6x2″), alternate potatoes with soup mixture. Top with wieners. Bake at 350°F. for 30 minutes. 4 servings.

SEAFOOD BAKE

1 can (10 fl. ounces) condensed
　cream of mushroom soup
⅓ cup salad dressing
⅓ cup milk
1 can (4 ¼ ounces) shrimp, drained
1 can (7 ounces) tuna or 1 can
　(5 ounces) crab, drained and
　flaked
1 can (5 ounces) water chestnuts,
　drained and sliced
1 cup finely diced celery
2 tablespoons chopped parsley
2 teaspoons grated onion
2 cups cooked macaroni
Paprika

In 1½-quart casserole, blend soup, salad dressing, and milk. Mix in all other ingredients except paprika (sprinkle it on top). Bake in a 350° oven 30 minutes or until hot. 4 to 6 servings.

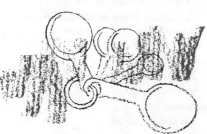

Meat Dishes Make the Meal

BEEF SPECIALTIES

Meat generally takes the largest part of the family food budget, and often makes the most important part of the meal. The smart homemaker can save time and put new flavour appeal into meat dishes, using canned condensed soups for cooking sauces. You will find new variety for family dinners in these easy, hearty beef dishes. Each has make-this-again flavour.

STEW 'N DUMPLINGS

1 can (14 ounces) whole onions, drained
1 tablespoon butter or margarine
1 can (10 fl. ounces) condensed vegetable soup
½ cup water
1½ cups diced cooked beef
1 cup prepared biscuit mix
⅓ cup milk

In saucepan, brown onions in butter. Add soup, water, and meat; heat. Meanwhile, combine biscuit mix and milk; drop by spoonfuls on hot stew making 8 dumplings. Cook uncovered 10 minutes and 10 minutes covered. 4 servings.

CREAMED COOKED BEEF

2 tablespoons chopped onion
1 tablespoon butter or margarine
1 can (10 fl. ounces) condensed cream of mushroom soup
½ cup water
1 cup diced cooked beef
½ cup cooked peas
Dash pepper
2 cups cooked noodles

Cook onion in butter until tender. Blend in soup and water; add beef, peas, and pepper. Heat; stir often. Serve over noodles. 3 to 4 servings.

SAUCY BEEF HASH

1 can (10 fl. ounces) condensed
   cream of celery soup
½ cup chopped parsley
¼ cup minced onion
1½ teaspoons Worcestershire
Dash pepper
2 cups diced cooked beef
2 cups diced cooked potatoes
2 tablespoons shortening
2 tablespoons milk

Combine ½ can soup, parsley, onion, 1 teaspoon Worcestershire, and pepper. Stir in beef and potatoes. In heavy frying pan, cook hash mixture in shortening over medium heat until browned. Meanwhile, combine remaining soup and Worcestershire with milk; heat and serve over hash. 4 servings.

SWISS STEAK WITH VEGETABLES

¼ cup flour
Dash pepper
1 pound round steak (½-inch thick)
2 tablespoons shortening
1 can (10 fl. ounces) condensed
   onion soup
½ cup water
4 medium carrots, cut in 2-inch
   pieces
4 medium potatoes, cut in half
1 tablespoon chopped parsley

Pound flour and pepper into steak with meat hammer or edge of heavy saucer. Cut into 4 serving pieces. In large frying pan, brown steak on both sides in shortening. Add soup, water, carrots, and potatoes. Cover; cook over low heat 45 minutes or until meat and vegetables are tender. Stir now and then. Sprinkle with parsley just before serving. 4 servings.

SPICY POT ROAST

3 to 4-pound beef pot roast
1 can (10 fl. ounces) condensed
   onion soup
¼ cup water
2 to 4 tablespoons flour

Brown meat well on all sides in heavy kettle; add soup. Cover; cook over low heat until meat is done—about 2½ to 3 hours. Remove meat; thicken gravy as desired, using a smooth paste made by blending water with flour. About 6 to 8 servings. (If desired, add vegetables—carrots, potatoes, turnips, etc—after meat has been cooking for 2 hours. Season. Cover; cook until vegetables are done—about 1 hour. Remove meat and vegetables to platter; thicken gravy according to directions.)

BARBECUED STEAK SUPREME

2 pounds steak (round or flank, ¾-inch thick)
2 tablespoons seasoned flour
2 tablespoons shortening
⅓ cup minced onion
⅓ cup minced celery
½ clove garlic, minced
1 can (10 fl. ounces) condensed tomato soup
2 tablespoons brown sugar
2 tablespoons Worcestershire
2 tablespoons lemon juice
2 teaspoons prepared mustard
Dash "Tabasco" sauce

Pound flour into steak. Brown in shortening in a heavy saucepan or frying pan, along with onion, celery, and garlic. Add remaining ingredients; stir well; cover. Cook in a 350° oven or on top of range for about 1½ hours or until tender. NOTE: Double all sauce ingredients for additional barbecue sauce to serve over fluffy rice or mashed potatoes. 6 servings.

SOUPER STROGANOFF

1 ½ pounds round steak, cut in thin strips
¼ cup flour
Dash pepper
¼ cup butter or margarine
⅓ cup canned sliced mushrooms, drained
½ cup chopped onion
1 small clove garlic, minced
1 can (10 fl. ounces) condensed consommé
1 cup sour cream
3 cups cooked noodles

Dust meat with flour and pepper. In frying pan, brown meat in butter. Add mushrooms, onion, and garlic; brown lightly. Stir in soup. Cover; cook 1 hour or until meat is tender; stir often. Gradually blend in sour cream; cook over low heat for 5 minutes. Serve over noodles. 4 servings.

SMOTHERED STEAK ROLL-UPS

1 ½ pounds thinly sliced round steak (¼ -inch thick)
1 ½ cups prepared packaged herb-seasoned stuffing
2 tablespoons shortening
1 can (10 fl. ounces) condensed cream of mushroom or golden mushroom soup
½ cup water

Cut steak into 6 pieces (about 8x 4"). Pound with meat hammer or edge of heavy saucer. Place ¼ cup stuffing near center of each piece of meat. Roll up; tuck in ends and fasten with skewers or toothpicks. In frying pan, brown roll-ups in shortening; pour off fat. Add soup and water. Cover; cook over low heat 1¼ hours or until tender. Stir now and then. 6 servings.

Meatball Stew Page 30
Norseman's Stew Page 27

TOMATO BEEF STEW

1 ½ pounds beef cubes
2 tablespoons shortening
1 can (10 fl. ounces) condensed
    tomato soup
½ cup water
6 small whole white onions
6 small carrots, cut in half
3 potatoes, quartered
¼ teaspoon whole thyme

Brown meat in shortening in large heavy pan. Add soup and water. Cover; simmer 1½ hours. Add remaining ingredients. Cover; cook 1 hour or until vegetables are tender. Stir now and then. To thicken, uncover; cook until desired consistency. 4 servings.

EASY SWISS STEAK

1 ½ pounds round steak
    (¾-inch thick)
2 tablespoons shortening
1 can (10 fl. ounces) condensed
    golden mushroom soup
½ cup chopped canned tomatoes
¼ cup chopped onion
¼ cup water
Dash pepper

Pound steak with meat hammer; cut into serving-size pieces. In frying pan, brown steak in shortening; pour off fat. Add remaining ingredients. Cover; cook over low heat 1 hour 15 minutes or until tender. Stir now and then. 4 to 6 servings.

NORSEMAN'S STEW

1 ½ pounds beef cubes (1 ½-inch)
2 tablespoons shortening
1 can (10 fl. ounces) condensed
    golden mushroom soup
½ cup water
½ cup chopped canned tomatoes
1 teaspoon wine vinegar
Generous dash cinnamon
2 whole cloves
1 pound (about 16) small whole
    white onions

In large heavy pan, brown beef in shortening; pour off fat. Stir in remaining ingredients except onions. Cover; cook over low heat 1½ hours. Add onions; cook 1 hour more or until meat is tender. Stir now and then. 4 servings.

wieners'n noodles page 11

CARNE QUISADA

¼ cup diced salt pork
1 ½ pounds beef cubes
1 teaspoon paprika
1 can (10 fl. ounces) condensed
   tomato soup
1 soup can water
1 medium onion, chopped (1 cup)
2 bay leaves
Dash red pepper
4 medium potatoes, peeled and
   quartered
1 teaspoon salt
10 pitted green olives
1 tablespoon capers, if desired
1 medium green pepper, chopped

Partially cook salt pork. Add beef and paprika; brown. Add soup, water, onion, bay leaves, and red pepper. Cover; cook over low heat about 1 hour 45 minutes. Add potatoes, salt, olives, and capers; cook 45 minutes longer or until potatoes are tender. Add green pepper last 15 minutes. Stir now and then. 8 servings.

STEAK IN SAUCE

¼ cup seasoned flour
1 ½ pounds round steak (about ¾-
   inch thick)
2 tablespoons shortening
1 can (10 fl. ounces) condensed
   cream of mushroom soup
½ soup can water
½ cup sour cream, if desired

Pound seasoned flour into steak with meat hammer or edge of heavy saucer. In large frying pan, brown steak on both sides in shortening. Add soup and water. Cover; cook over low heat 45 minutes or until steak is tender. Stir often. Just before serving stir in sour cream. 4 to 6 servings.

SPICY SHORT RIBS

3 pounds short ribs of beef
¼ cup flour
2 tablespoons shortening
1 can (10 fl. ounces) condensed
   beef broth
1 cup dried apricots or prunes
2 tablespoons brown sugar
2 tablespoons vinegar
¼ teaspoon ground cinnamon
¼ teaspoon ground cloves
¼ teaspoon ground allspice

Dust ribs with flour; brown in shortening in large heavy pan. Pour off excess drippings. Combine remaining ingredients; pour over ribs. Cover; cook over low heat 2½ hours or until ribs are tender; turn ribs and baste with sauce often. 4 to 6 servings.

STROGANOFF STEW

3 ½-pound boned chuck roast
2 tablespoons shortening
2 cans (10 fl. ounces each)
    condensed cream of mushroom
    soup
½ cup sour cream
½ cup water
1 teaspoon paprika
Generous dash pepper
1 pound medium carrots, halved
1 pound whole small white onions
Cooked wide noodles

Trim fat from meat and cut into 1-inch cubes. In large heavy pan, brown beef in shortening; pour off fat. Add soup, sour cream, water, paprika, and pepper. Cover; cook over low heat 1 hour. Stir now and then. Add vegetables. Cover; cook over low heat 1 hour longer or until meat and vegetables are tender. Stir now and then. Serve with noodles. 6 servings.

CORNED BEEF 'N CABBAGE CASSEROLE

1 can (10 fl. ounces) condensed
    cream of celery soup
½ cup chopped onion
1 teaspoon dry mustard
1 cup diced cooked corned beef
4 cups coarsely shredded cabbage

Mix all ingredients in 1½-quart casserole. Cover; bake in a 375° oven 45 minutes. 3 to 4 servings.

PEPPER STEAK

1 ½ pounds round steak (about
    ¾-inch thick)
2 tablespoons shortening
1 can (10 fl. ounces) condensed
    tomato soup
⅓ cup water
1 teaspoon lemon juice
½ cup green pepper strips

Pound steak with hammer or edge of heavy saucer. In frying pan, brown meat in shortening; pour off fat. Stir in soup, water, and lemon juice. Cover; cook over low heat 1 hour 15 minutes. Add pepper. Cook 15 minutes more or until meat is tender. Stir now and then. 4 to 6 servings.

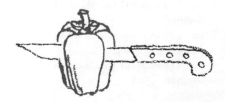

HAMBURGER 15 WAYS

Ground beef makes economy meals with good flavour the whole family enjoys—especially when the meat is seasoned with the addition of soup. Soup prevents shrinkage in meat loaves and burgers; stretches food values while it adds good taste.

SPREAD-A-BURGER

1   can (10 fl. ounces) condensed
    tomato soup
1 ½   pounds ground beef
⅓   cup finely chopped onion
1   tablespoon prepared mustard
1   tablespoon Worcestershire
1   teaspoon salt
1   teaspoon prepared horseradish
Dash pepper
8   wiener buns, split and toasted
8   slices (8 ounces) process Cheddar
    cheese

Combine ⅓ cup soup with remaining ingredients except buns and cheese. Spread mixture evenly over bun halves; *cover edges completely.* Broil 3 to 4 inches from heat for 5 minutes or until done. Top with remaining soup and cheese. Broil until cheese melts. Makes 8 sandwiches.

MEATBALL STEW

1 ½   pounds ground beef
1   egg, slightly beaten
1   cup small bread cubes
¼   cup finely chopped onion
1   teaspoon salt
2   tablespoons shortening
1   can (10 fl. ounces) condensed
    beef broth
1   can (10 fl. ounces) condensed
    tomato soup
¼   teaspoon thyme, crushed
1   can (14 ounces) sliced carrots,
    drained
1   can (19 ounces) whole white
    potatoes, drained
1   can (14 ounces) whole onions,
    drained

Mix beef, egg, bread, onion, and salt; shape into 24 meatballs. Brown in shortening in frying pan; pour off fat. Add remaining ingredients. Cook over low heat 20 min.; stir now and then. Top with chopped parsley. 6 servings.

OLD-FASHIONED MEAT LOAF

1 can (10 fl. ounces) condensed
   vegetable soup
2 pounds ground beef
½ cup chopped onion
½ cup fine dry bread crumbs
1 egg, slightly beaten
1 teaspoon salt
Dash pepper

Combine all ingredients; mix thoroughly. Shape *firmly* into loaf (8x4x2½"); place in shallow baking pan. (*Thorough* mixing and *firm* shaping will produce a moist, easy-to-slice loaf.) Bake at 350°F. about 1½ hours. 6 servings. VARIATION: After loaf has baked 1¼ hours, garnish top with 4 tomato slices and ½ cup shredded mild cheese; bake 15 minutes more.

TOP-STOVE MEAT LOAF

1½ pounds ground beef
½ cup dry bread crumbs
1 can (10 fl. ounces) condensed
   tomato soup
¼ cup finely chopped onion
1 egg, slightly beaten
1 teaspoon salt
Generous dash pepper
1 tablespoon shortening
¼ cup water
½ teaspoon prepared mustard
2 slices process cheese, cut in half

Thoroughly mix beef, crumbs, ¼ cup soup, onion, egg, and seasonings. Shape *firmly* into 2 loaves; brown on both sides in frying pan in shortening (to turn loaves, use pancake turner). Cover; cook over low heat 25 minutes. Spoon off fat. Stir in remaining soup, water, mustard. Top loaves with cheese. Uncover; cook 10 minutes. 4 to 6 servings. *Oven Method:* Mix and shape as above. Bake at 350°F. for 40 minutes. Spoon off fat. Pour remaining soup (omit water) mixed with mustard on loaves; top with cheese. Bake 5 minutes more.

SPAGHETTI WITH MEAT SAUCE

1 pound ground beef
1 to 2 cloves garlic, minced
1 cup chopped onion
2 cans (10 fl. ounces each) condensed tomato soup
½ soup can water
1 teaspoon salt
1 bay leaf
⅛ teaspoon pepper
⅛ teaspoon leaf thyme
16 ounces thin spaghetti, cooked

Brown beef, garlic, and onion. Blend in soup, water, and seasonings. Simmer 30 minutes; stir often. Serve sauce over spaghetti; sprinkle with grated Parmesan cheese. 4 servings.

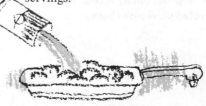

ONION BURGERS

1 pound ground beef
1 cup chopped celery
1 tablespoon shortening
1 can (10 fl. ounces) condensed
  onion soup
½ cup water
¼ cup ketchup
1 teaspoon Worcestershire
1 teaspoon prepared mustard
Dash pepper
6 buns, toasted and buttered

Brown beef with celery in shortening; stir to separate meat particles. Add soup, water, and seasonings. Simmer 10 to 15 minutes or until slightly thickened. Stir now and then. Serve on buns. 6 servings.

HAMBURGERS ITALIANO

1 pound ground beef
½ teaspoon salt
Dash pepper
¼ cup canned sliced mushrooms,
  drained
1 small onion, sliced
⅛ teaspoon leaf oregano, crushed
1 small clove garlic, minced
2 tablespoons butter or margarine
1 can (10 fl. ounces) condensed
  tomato soup
¼ cup water

Combine beef, salt, and pepper; shape into 4 hamburgers. Brown hamburgers along with mushrooms, onion, oregano, and garlic in butter. Stir in soup and water. Cover; cook over low heat 15 minutes; stir often. 4 servings.

MEAT-SHELL PIE

1 can (10 fl. ounces) condensed
  tomato soup
1½ pounds ground beef
1 teaspoon salt
1½ teaspoons chili powder
6 wieners, split
½ cup chopped onion
2 tablespoons butter or margarine
½ cup shredded process cheese
Grated parmesan cheese

Place a double layer of foil on cookie sheet. Mix thoroughly ⅓ cup soup, beef, salt, and 1 teaspoon chili powder; pat out firmly into 11-inch circle about ½-inch thick on foil. Turn up edges of foil to catch fat. Firmly press wieners, cut side up, into meat in spoke fashion. In saucepan, cook onion with remaining chili in butter until tender; stir in remaining soup; spread over meat. Bake at 450°F. for 15 minutes. Spoon off fat. Sprinkle with cheeses, bake until melted. 6 servings.

MANY WAY MEATBALLS

1 pound ground beef
¼ cup dry bread crumbs
¼ cup minced onion
1 egg, slightly beaten
¼ teaspoon salt
1 can (10 fl. ounces) condensed
   Cheddar cheese, cream of celery
   or mushroom soup
½ cup water
2 tablespoons chopped parsley

Mix beef, bread crumbs, onion, egg, and salt; shape into 16 meatballs. In frying pan, brown meatballs; pour off drippings. Stir in soup, water, and parsley. Cover; cook over low heat 20 minutes; stir often. 4 servings.

STUFFED CABBAGE ROLLS

8 large cabbage leaves
1 pound ground beef
1 cup cooked rice
¼ cup chopped onion
1 egg, slightly beaten
1 teaspoon salt
¼ teaspoon pepper
1 can (10 fl. ounces) condensed
   tomato soup

Cook cabbage leaves in boiling salted water a few minutes to soften; drain. Combine beef, rice, onion, egg, salt, and pepper with 2 tablespoons soup. Divide meat mixture among cabbage leaves; roll and secure with toothpicks or string. Place cabbage rolls in frying pan; pour remaining soup over. Cover; cook over low heat about 40 minutes. Stir often, spooning sauce over rolls. 4 servings.

SOUPER SAUCY MEAT LOAF

1½ pounds ground beef
1 can (10 fl. ounces) condensed
   cream of mushroom or
   tomato soup
1 cup small bread cubes
¼ cup finely chopped onion
1 egg, slightly beaten
½ teaspoon salt
Generous dash pepper
¼ cup water

Mix *thoroughly* beef, ½ cup soup, bread, onion, egg, salt, and pepper. Shape *firmly* into loaf; place in shallow ′baking pan. Bake at 350°F. for 1 hour 15 minutes. Blend remaining soup, water, and 2 to 3 tablespoons drippings. Heat; stir now and then. Serve over loaf. 4 to 6 servings.

ROLL-IN-ONE MEAT LOAF

1 can (10 fl. ounces) condensed
    tomato soup
1 ½ pounds ground beef
½ cup fine dry bread crumbs
¼ cup minced onion
2 tablespoons chopped parsley
1 egg, slightly beaten
1 teaspoon salt
Dash pepper
1 package (10 ounces) frozen cut
    green beans, cooked, well drained

Combine ½ cup soup with all ingredients except beans. Mix well. On waxed paper, pat into a 12x9-inch shape. Spread beans to within 1 inch of all edges; pat into meat. With aid of waxed paper, roll meat tightly, jelly-roll fashion, starting at long edge. Seal ends; use waxed paper to transfer to baking dish. Bake at 350°F. for 40 minutes. Spoon off fat. Pour remaining soup over loaf. Bake 10 minutes longer. 6 servings.

SWEDISH MEATBALLS

1 pound ground beef
¼ cup fine dry bread crumbs
¼ cup minced onion
1 egg, slightly beaten
2 tablespoons chopped parsley
1 can (10 fl. ounces) condensed
    cream of celery soup
½ soup can water
1 to 2 tablespoons finely chopped
    dill pickle
Cooked rice

Mix beef, bread crumbs, onion, egg, and parsley; shape into 24 meatballs. In frying pan, brown meatballs; pour off drippings. Stir in soup, water, and pickle. Cover; cook over low heat 20 minutes; stir often. Serve with rice. 4 servings.

STUFFED PEPPERS

4 medium green peppers
1 pound ground beef
½ cup chopped onion
1 tablespoon butter or margarine
1 can (10 fl. ounces) condensed
    tomato soup
1 cup cooked rice
1 teaspoon Worcestershire
½ teaspoon salt
Dash pepper

Remove tops and seeds from peppers; cook in boiling salted water about 5 minutes; drain. Brown beef and cook onion in butter until tender; stir in 1 cup soup and remaining ingredients. Spoon meat mixture into peppers; place in 1½-quart casserole. Bake in a 375° oven 30 minutes. Heat remaining soup and serve over peppers. 4 servings.

SAVOURY SHEPHERD'S PIE

1 pound ground beef
¼ cup chopped onion
¼ cup chopped green pepper
1 can (10 fl. ounces) condensed
   vegetable soup
¼ teaspoon salt
Dash thyme, if desired
Seasoned mashed potatoes (about
   1 cup)

Brown beef and cook onion and green pepper until tender; stir in soup, salt, and thyme. Spoon into 1-quart casserole; place potatoes in mounds around edge of casserole. Bake in a 425° oven 15 minutes. 4 servings.

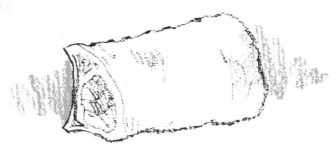

PORK TO PERFECTION

Do you make the most of the good pork values often available in the markets? Condensed soups add new colour and flavour to thrifty pork dishes, rich in proteins and B-vitamins. Here are some recipes to help you make varied new main dishes of ham and pork.

BARBECUED LOIN OF PORK

3- to 5-pound loin (or shoulder) of
   pork
1 can (10 fl. ounces) condensed
   tomato soup
⅓ cup chopped onion
⅓ cup chopped celery
1 clove garlic, minced
2 tablespoons brown sugar
2 tablespoons Worcestershire
2 tablespoons lemon juice or
   vinegar
2 teaspoons prepared mustard
4 drops "Tabasco" sauce

Roast pork in shallow pan at 325° about 45 minutes per pound. One hour before meat is done, pour off drippings. Combine soup and remaining ingredients to make sauce. Pour over meat; continue roasting; spoon sauce over meat often.

GLAZED FRUITED PORK CHOPS

4 pork chops (about 1 pound)
4 slices apple
4 slices orange
Dash ground cinnamon
Dash ground cloves
1 can (10 fl. ounces) condensed
   beef broth
1 tablespoon brown sugar
2 tablespoons orange juice
1 tablespoon cornstarch

Brown chops on both sides; pour off drippings. Place an apple and orange slice on each chop; sprinkle with cinnamon and cloves. Add soup and sugar. Cover; cook over low heat 35 minutes. Mix orange juice and cornstarch until smooth; gradually blend into soup. Cook; stir constantly until slightly thickened; simmer a few minutes or until chops are tender. 3 to 4 servings.

HAM BAKE

1 cup diced cooked ham
2 tablespoons chopped onion
⅛ teaspoon tarragon
2 tablespoons butter or margarine
1 can (10 fl. ounces) condensed
   cream of chicken soup
½ cup water
1½ cups cooked noodles
½ cup cooked French style green
   beans
2 tablespoons fine dry bread crumbs
½ small clove garlic, minced

Cook ham, onion, and tarragon in 1 tablespoon butter until ham is browned and onion is tender. Stir in soup, water, noodles, and green beans. Pour into buttered 1-quart casserole. Lightly brown crumbs and garlic in remaining tablespoon butter; sprinkle over top of casserole. Bake in a 350° oven 30 minutes or until hot and bubbly. 3 to 4 servings.

HURRY-UP PORK HASH

1 medium onion, thinly sliced
2 tablespoons butter or margarine
1 can (10 fl. ounces) condensed
   cream of celery or mushroom soup
½ cup milk
1 teaspoon Worcestershire
1 cup cubed cooked pork
1 cup cubed cooked potatoes
   (about 2 medium)
½ cup cooked peas
Dash pepper

Cook onion in butter until lightly browned. Blend in soup, milk, and Worcestershire. Add remaining ingredients. Cook over low heat 10 minutes; stir often. 2 to 3 servings.

GLORIFIED CHOPS

6 pork chops (about 1½ pounds)
1 can (10 fl. ounces) condensed
cream of celery, mushroom, or
tomato soup
¼ to ⅓ cup water

In frying pan, brown chops. Pour off fat. Stir in soup, water. Cover, cook over low heat 45 minutes or until tender. Stir now and then. 4 servings.

CREAMY BAKED CHOPS

Brown chops in oven-proof pan as above. After adding liquids, cover; bake at 350°F. for 1 hour or until tender.

PORK CHOPS 'N STUFFING

4 pork chops (about 1 pound)
3 cups soft bread cubes
2 tablespoons chopped onion
¼ cup melted butter or margarine
¼ cup water
¼ teaspoon poultry seasoning
1 can (10 fl. ounces) condensed
cream of mushroom soup
⅓ cup water

Brown chops on both sides; place in shallow baking dish. Lightly mix together bread cubes, onion, butter, ¼ cup water and poultry seasoning. Place a mound of stuffing on each chop. Blend soup and ⅓ cup water; pour over. Bake in a 350° oven 1 hour or until tender. 3 to 4 servings.

PORK CHOP AND POTATO SCALLOP

4 pork chops (about 1 pound)
1 can (10 fl. ounces) condensed
cream of mushroom soup
½ cup sour cream
¼ cup water
2 tablespoons chopped parsley
4 cups thinly sliced potatoes
Salt
Pepper

Brown chops. Blend soup, sour cream, water, and parsley. In 2-quart casserole, alternate layers of potatoes sprinkled with salt and pepper, and sauce. Top with chops. Cover; bake in a 375° oven 1¼ hours. 3 to 4 servings.

LAMB, VEAL, LIVER

Many Canadian housewives repeat their complete range of main dish recipes every two weeks. You can find new mealtime variety and interest in more extensive use of these special meats. Try stewing lamb in savoury soup sauce; add zest to veal dishes seasoned quickly and easily with a can of soup. Discover new flavour in nutritious liver simmered in flavourful sauces.

LAMB KABOBS

¼ cup chopped onion
1 clove garlic, minced
1 teaspoon curry powder
⅛ teaspoon ground ginger
2 tablespoons butter or margarine
1 can (10 fl. ounces) condensed cream of mushroom soup
¼ cup water
1 pound leg of lamb, cut in 1½-inch cubes
2 apples, quartered
1 medium green pepper, cut in 1½-inch pieces
8 small white onions

For sauce, cook onion, garlic, curry powder, and ginger in butter until onion is tender. Add soup and water; cook 5 minutes; stir often. (Partially precook green pepper and white onions if very tender vegetables are desired.) On 4 skewers, alternate lamb, apple, green pepper, and onion; place on broiler rack. Brush kabobs with sauce. Broil, about 4 inches from heat, for 30 minutes or until meat is tender; turn kabobs and brush with sauce every 5 minutes. 4 servings.

MUSHROOM-LAMB CURRY

½ cup chopped onion
½ cup chopped green pepper
½ cup chopped celery
1 large clove garlic, minced
¼ cup butter or margarine
1 pound lamb cubes
2 teaspoons curry powder
1 can (10 fl. ounces) condensed cream of mushroom soup
1 cup water
3 cups cooked rice

Cook onion, green pepper, celery, and garlic in butter until vegetables are tender; push to side of pan. Add lamb; brown with curry powder. Blend in soup and water. Cover; cook over low heat 1 hour or until tender; stir often. Serve over rice. 4 servings.

GRANDMOTHER'S LAMB STEW

1 pound lamb cubes
1 large clove garlic, minced
¼ teaspoon leaf thyme, crushed
2 tablespoons butter or margarine
1 can (10 fl. ounces) condensed
   onion soup
½ soup can water
1 cup diced celery
½ cup cooked tomatoes
½ teaspoon salt
¼ teaspoon pepper
4 medium potatoes (about 1
   pound), quartered
1 package (10 ounces) frozen cut
   green beans

Cook lamb, garlic, and thyme in butter in large heavy pan until lamb is browned. Add soup, water, celery, tomatoes, and seasonings. Cover; cook over low heat about 1 hour. Add potatoes; cover; cook 20 minutes. Add green beans; cover; cook 15 minutes more; stir often. 4 servings.

LAMB RAGOUT

1½ pounds lamb cubes
2 tablespoons flour
¼ cup shortening
1 can (10 fl. ounces) condensed
   tomato soup
1 soup can water
1 teaspoon salt
⅛ teaspoon pepper
1 clove garlic, minced
⅛ to ¼ teaspoon caraway seed
   (optional)
3 medium potatoes, quartered
   (about 2 cups)
½ medium cabbage, cut in wedges

Dust lamb with flour; brown in shortening in large heavy kettle or pot. Add soup, water, salt, pepper, garlic, and caraway seed. Cover; simmer 1 hour; stir often. Add potatoes to broth; cover and cook 15 minutes. Lay cabbage on top. Cover; cook 30 minutes more or until meat and vegetables are tender. 4 to 6 servings.

VIENNA VEAL AND NOODLES

1½ pounds veal cubes
1 clove garlic, minced
¼ teaspoon marjoram (optional)
2 tablespoons butter or margarine
1 can (10 fl. ounces) condensed
   cream of mushroom soup
½ soup can water
¼ teaspoon paprika
Cooked noodles

In oven-proof pan, brown veal, garlic, and marjoram in butter. Blend in soup, water, and paprika. Cover; bake in a 350° oven 1 hour or until tender. Serve with hot noodles. 4 to 6 servings.

VEAL GOULASH

1 pound veal steak (½-inch thick)
2 tablespoons shortening
1 cup sliced mushrooms
¼ cup finely chopped onion
1 can (10 fl. ounces) condensed
   tomato soup
½ cup sour cream
¼ cup water
1 bay leaf
½ teaspoon salt
¼ teaspoon pepper
1 teaspoon paprika
Cooked rice

Cut veal into 4 pieces. Brown well on both sides in shortening. Add mushrooms and onion; cook until lightly browned. Blend in remaining ingredients except rice. Cover; simmer 45 minutes or until meat is tender; stir often. Remove bay leaf before serving. Serve over rice. 4 servings.

VEAL BIRDS

1 pound thinly sliced veal cutlet
1 cup cooked rice
2 tablespoons butter or margarine
2 tablespoons chopped parsley
2 tablespoons shortening
2 tablespoons chopped onion
1 can (10 fl. ounces) condensed old
   fashioned tomato rice soup
¼ cup water
⅛ teaspoon oregano, if desired

Pound veal with meat hammer; cut into 4 large or 8 small pieces. Combine rice, butter, and parsley; place a small amount on each piece of veal; roll and fasten with toothpicks or skewers. Brown veal birds in shortening along with onion; pour off excess drippings. Combine remaining ingredients; pour over meat. Cover; cook over low heat for 45 minutes. Spoon sauce over meat occasionally. 4 servings. Thin sauce to desired consistency with small amount of water before serving.

SAVOURY LIVER

1 pound thinly sliced liver, cut in
   strips
2 tablespoons flour
½ medium green pepper, sliced
1 medium onion, sliced
¼ cup shortening
1 can (10 fl. ounces) condensed
   tomato soup
¼ cup water
1 to 2 thin slices lemon, cut in
   quarters

Dust liver with flour. Brown with green pepper and onion in shortening. Add soup, water, and lemon. Cover; cook over low heat 30 minutes or until liver is tender. Stir often. 4 servings.

LIVER INDIENNE

½ pound chicken livers
½ cup sliced celery
⅓ cup chopped onion
1 teaspoon curry powder
2 tablespoons butter or margarine
1 can (10 fl. ounces) condensed
   golden mushroom soup
⅓ cup water
Cooked rice

In saucepan, cook livers, celery, onion, and curry in butter until livers are done. Stir in soup and water. Heat; stir now and then. Serve over rice. 2 servings.

CHILI LIVER

4 slices bacon
1 pound sliced beef or calves liver
2 tablespoons flour
1 can (10 fl. ounces) condensed
   onion soup
¼ cup chili sauce or ketchup

In frying pan, cook bacon until crisp; remove and crumble. Pour off fat, reserving 2 tablespoons drippings. Dust liver with flour; brown in drippings. Add soup and chili sauce. Cover; cook over low heat 30 minutes or until tender. Stir now and then. Uncover; cook to desired consistency. Garnish with bacon. 4 servings.

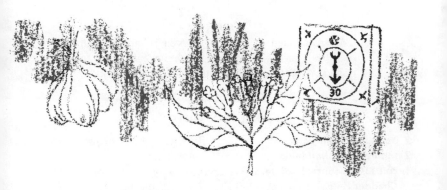

Poultry

There is new versatility to cooking poultry. With chicken parts readily available, either fresh or frozen, and canned chicken handy for hurry-up dinners, chicken comes to the table more often than ever.

You can add to your ways of preparing chicken thanks to flavourful soup sauces. From Glorified Chicken to Poulet au Vin here is an international range of quick and easy dishes.

Turkey now comes to the table more often, too. When a large turkey makes its second-act appearance, give it a dramatic switch in flavour and appearance. Choose from Turkey Divan to an easy à la king dish, ready in minutes.

TURKEY
Where cooked or canned chicken is indicated in recipes, turkey may be used instead. Frozen chicken parts are to be thawed before cooking.

GLORIFIED CHICKEN

2 **pounds chicken parts**
2 **tablespoons shortening**
1 **can (10 fl. ounces) condensed Cheddar cheese, cream of celery, chicken, or mushroom soup**

In frying pan, brown chicken in shortening. Pour off fat. Stir in soup. Cover; cook over low heat 45 minutes or until tender. Stir now and then. 4 servings.

PENTHOUSE CHICKEN

2 pounds chicken parts
¼ cup seasoned flour
Shortening or salad oil
½ medium green pepper, cut in strips
½ cup sliced onion
⅛ to ¼ teaspoon thyme
1 can (10 fl. ounces) condensed tomato soup
¼ cup water
1 teaspoon vinegar

Dust chicken with seasoned flour. Brown in frying pan in hot shortening (¼-inch deep). Cover; cook over low heat 45 minutes. Uncover last 10 minutes to crisp. Remove chicken to heated platter; keep warm. Pour off all but 2 tablespoons fat. Add green pepper, onion, and thyme; cook until green pepper is tender. Add remaining ingredients. Heat; stir now and then. Serve over chicken. 4 to 6 servings.

ONE-STEP METHOD:

Omit flour and water. Brown chicken in 2 tablespoons shortening. Pour off fat. Sprinkle with salt, pepper. Add remaining ingredients (increase vinegar to 1 tablespoon). Cover; cook over low heat 45 minutes or until tender. Stir now and then.

DREAMY CHICKEN STEW

1 can (10 fl. ounces) condensed cream of chicken soup
1½ cups water
1 cup sliced celery
1 medium onion, quartered
1 teaspoon salt
¼ teaspoon poultry seasoning
⅛ teaspoon pepper
1 stewing chicken (4 to 5 pounds), cut up
4 medium potatoes (about 1 pound), quartered
6 medium carrots, cut in pieces
¼ cup flour

Combine soup, 1 cup water, celery, onion, and seasonings in large heavy pan; add chicken. Cover; cook over low heat 1½ hours; stir often. Add vegetables. Cover; cook 45 minutes or until chicken and vegetables are tender. To thicken, blend flour and remaining water; gradually stir into stew. Cook 10 to 15 minutes; stir often. 4 to 6 servings.

TURKEY DIVAN
(also Chicken Divan)

1 package (10 ounces) frozen broccoli or asparagus spears, cooked and drained
4 large slices chicken or turkey
1 can (10 fl. ounces) condensed cream of celery, chicken, or mushroom soup
⅓ cup milk
½ cup shredded Canadian Cheddar cheese

Arrange broccoli in shallow baking dish (10 x 6 x 2"). Top with turkey slices. Blend soup and milk; pour over turkey; sprinkle with cheese. Bake in a 450° oven until sauce is slightly browned, about 15 minutes. 4 servings.

POULET AU VIN

2 pounds chicken parts
¼ cup butter or margarine
1 can (10 fl. ounces) condensed
    cream of mushroom soup
⅓ cup sherry (optional)
Dash pepper
10 small white onions

Brown chicken in butter in large frying pan. Stir in soup, sherry, and pepper; add onions. Cover; simmer 45 minutes or until chicken is tender; stir often. 4 to 6 servings. (If desired, add ⅛ teaspoon whole thyme when browning chicken and substitute ⅓ cup water for sherry. Omit pepper.)

GOLDEN CHICKEN BAKE

2 pounds chicken parts
2 tablespoons melted butter or
    margarine
1 can (10 fl. ounces) condensed
    Cheddar cheese, cream of celery,
    chicken, or mushroom soup
¼ cup chopped toasted almonds

In shallow baking dish (12x8x2"), arrange chicken skin-side down. Pour butter over. Bake at 400°F. for 20 minutes. Turn chicken; bake 20 minutes more. Stir soup; pour over chicken; sprinkle with almonds. Bake 20 minutes more or until tender. Stir sauce before serving. 4 servings.

CHICKEN CROQUETTES WITH SAUCE

1 can (10 fl. ounces) condensed
    cream of chicken soup
1½ cups minced cooked chicken
¼ cup fine dry bread crumbs
2 tablespoons minced parsley
1 tablespoon finely minced onion
Shortening
¼ cup milk

Combine ⅓ cup soup with chicken, ¼ cup crumbs, parsley, and onion. Form into 6 croquettes; roll in bread crumbs. Chill. Fry croquettes in shortening until thoroughly heated and lightly browned. Blend remaining soup with milk; heat; serve over croquettes. 3 servings.

CREAMED CHICKEN

½ cup chopped celery
2 tablespoons butter or margarine
1 can (10 fl. ounces) condensed
    cream of chicken soup
⅓ to ½ cup milk
1 can (6 ounces) boned chicken or
    1 cup diced cooked chicken or
    turkey
1 cup cooked peas
⅛ teaspoon ground sage

Cook celery in butter until tender. Blend in other ingredients. Heat; stir often. Serve over biscuits, or toast. 3 servings.

CHICKEN À LA KING

¼ cup chopped onion
2 tablespoons chopped green pepper
2 tablespoons butter or margarine
1 can (10 fl. ounces) condensed cream of chicken or mushroom soup
⅓ to ½ cup milk
1 ½ cups cubed cooked chicken, ham, or turkey
2 tablespoons diced pimiento
Dash pepper
Toast

Cook onion and green pepper in butter until tender. Blend in soup and milk; add chicken, pimiento, and pepper. Heat slowly; stir often. Serve over toast. 3 to 4 servings.

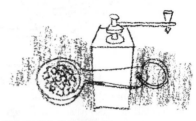

CHICKEN LIVERS IN PATTY SHELLS

½ pound chicken livers
2 tablespoons butter or margarine
½ cup chopped celery
¼ cup chopped onion
1 can (10 fl. ounces) condensed cream of chicken or mushroom soup
⅓ cup milk
¼ teaspoon paprika
Patty shells

Cook livers slowly in butter or margarine in covered pan until thawed and browned; stir often. Add celery and onion; cook until tender. Gradually blend in soup, milk, and paprika. Heat; stir often. Serve in patty shells. 2 to 3 servings.

PARTY CHICKEN

2 pounds chicken parts
2 tablespoons shortening
1 can (10 fl. ounces) condensed chicken with rice soup
½ cup canned mushroom buttons, drained
⅓ cup Burgundy or other dry red wine
10 small whole white onions
1 bay leaf
1 large clove garlic, minced
¼ teaspoon thyme, crushed
½ cup water
¼ cup flour
Chopped parsley

In frying pan, brown chicken in shortening; pour off fat. Add soup, mushrooms, wine, onions, bay leaf, garlic, and thyme. Cover; cook over low heat 45 minutes or until chicken and onions are tender. Stir now and then. Remove bay leaf. Gradually blend water into flour until smooth; slowly stir into sauce. Cook, stirring until thickened. Garnish with parsley. 4 servings.

Savoury Stuffings

Whether in a holiday turkey, large roasting chicken, or a fresh or frozen fish, stuffing glorifies a hearty main dish, and makes a feast. It's the cook's secret that this moist and flavourful family favourite is thrifty, too.

OLD-FASHIONED POULTRY STUFFING

8 cups bread cubes
1 cup chopped celery
½ cup finely chopped onion
¼ to ½ teaspoon poultry seasoning
Dash pepper
¼ cup butter or margarine
1 can (10 fl. ounces) condensed cream of celery, chicken, or mushroom soup

Brown bread cubes on cookie sheet at 350°F. for 5 minutes. In frying pan, cook celery and onion with seasonings in butter until vegetables are tender. Add soup; mix lightly with bread. Spoon into 1½-quart casserole. Bake at 350°F. for 45 minutes. Makes 6 cups stuffing.

OVERSTUFFED CHICKEN

2 cans (10 fl. ounces each) condensed golden mushroom soup
⅔ cup water
1 package (8½ fl. ounces) seasoned stuffing
2 broilers (about 2½ pounds each), split
Paprika
⅓ cup chopped onion
Generous dash poultry seasoning
2 tablespoons butter or margarine

Combine soup with water. In roasting pan (15x10½"), mix 2/3 cup soup mixture with stuffing mix; spread in pan. Arrange broilers over stuffing, sprinkle with paprika. Cover; bake at 400°F. for 30 minutes. Uncover, bake 45 minutes longer or until tender. Meanwhile, in saucepan, cook onion with seasoning in butter until onion is tender. Stir in remaining soup mixture. Heat; stir now and then. Serve with chicken and stuffing. 4 servings.

OYSTER BAR STUFFING

¼ cup chopped celery
2 tablespoons chopped onion
¼ teaspoon sage
2 tablespoons butter or margarine
1 can (10 fl. ounces) condensed
   oyster stew
8 cups dried bread cubes

In saucepan, cook celery and onion with sage in butter until tender. Add soup. Toss lightly with bread cubes. Spoon into 1½-quart casserole. Bake at 350°F. for 45 minutes. Makes about 4 cups stuffing.

SAVOURY SAUSAGE STUFFING

½ pound sausage
1 small onion, chopped
1 can (10 fl. ounces) condensed
   cream of celery soup
8 cups dry bread cubes

Brown sausage; stir to separate meat particles. (If using link sausage, slice before browning.) Add onion; cook until tender. Blend in soup; mix lightly with bread cubes. Makes about 6 cups stuffing, or enough for a 5-to 6-pound bird.

HOLIDAY STUFFING

½ cup chopped onion
2 cups chopped celery
6 tablespoons butter or margarine
5 cups corn bread crumbs (one 12-ounce package corn muffin mix, baked as directed)
3 cups dry bread cubes
1 teaspoon poultry seasoning
1 can (10 fl. ounces) condensed
   cream of chicken soup
¼ cup milk

Cook onion and celery in butter until tender. Combine with corn bread crumbs, bread cubes, and poultry seasoning. Blend soup and milk; pour over bread mixture; mix lightly. Makes about 8 cups stuffing or enough for an 8- to 10-pound turkey.

DUTCH COUNTRY STUFFING

1 can (10 fl. ounces) condensed
   beef broth
2 cups chopped apple
¾ cup chopped onion
½ cup chopped celery
¼ cup sugar
2 tablespoons butter or margarine
¼ teaspoon ground sage
⅛ teaspoon ground nutmeg
Dash ground cinnamon
12 cups dry bread cubes

Combine all ingredients except bread cubes; simmer 10 minutes. Pour over bread cubes a little at a time, mixing well after each addition. Makes about 8 cups or enough stuffing for a 5- to 6-pound pork shoulder roast.

Fish and Seafood

Fish never tastes better than when brought to the table bubbling in a savoury sauce.

Whether you catch your fish in the freezer or offshore, you can give it family-appeal flavour and extra colour by these recipes. They include budget balancers and party spectaculars you'll treasure.

SAUCY FISH FILLETS

1 pound fish fillets
Generous dash pepper
1 can (10 fl. ounces) condensed
　cream of celery soup
½ cup shredded mild process cheese
Generous dash paprika

Arrange fillets in single layer in shallow baking dish (10x6x2"); sprinkle with pepper. Bake at 350°F. for 15 minutes. Pour soup over, stirring into liquid around fish. Sprinkle with cheese and paprika. Bake 10 minutes more or until done. Stir before serving. Garnish with parsley or lemon wedges if desired. 3 servings.

SEASIDE STEW

½ cup sliced mushrooms, drained
1 tablespoon butter or margarine
1 can (10 fl. ounces) condensed
　cream of celery soup
½ cup milk
2 cups diced cooked seafood
　(crabmeat, shrimp, scallops,
　whitefish)
¼ cup shredded sharp Canadian
Cheddar cheese
3 tablespoons sauterne or other
　dry white wine

In saucepan, brown mushrooms in butter. Add remaining ingredients. Heat until cheese melts; stir now and then. Serve over rice. Garnish with paprika and parsley. 4 to 6 servings.

SHRIMP À LA KING

½ cup sliced mushrooms, drained
¼ cup chopped onion
2 tablespoons butter or margarine
1 can (10 fl. ounces) condensed
Cheddar cheese soup
½ cup milk
1 cup diced cooked shrimp
Rice or toast

In saucepan, brown mushrooms and cook onion in butter until tender. Add soup, milk, and shrimp. Heat; stir now and then. Serve over rice. 3 servings.

SHRIMP CREOLE

1 large green pepper, sliced
1 large onion, sliced
1 small clove garlic, minced
2 tablespoons shortening
1 can (10 fl. ounces) condensed
tomato soup
⅓ cup water
2 teaspoons lemon juice
¼ teaspoon salt
Dash pepper
Dash "Tabasco" sauce
1 pound shrimp, cooked and
cleaned (or three 4½ ounce
cans, drained)
3 cups cooked rice

Cook green pepper, onion, and garlic in shortening in covered frying pan over low heat until tender. Stir in soup, water, lemon juice, seasonings, and shrimp. Cook about 10 minutes; stir often. Serve over rice. 4 to 6 servings.

LOBSTER-SHRIMP THERMIDOR

½ cup sliced mushrooms, drained
1 tablespoon butter or margarine
1 can (10 fl. ounces) condensed
cream of celery soup
¼ cup milk
1 cup diced cooked lobster
½ cup diced cooked shrimp
¼ teaspoon dry mustard
Dash cayenne pepper
Grated Parmesan cheese
Paprika

In saucepan, brown mushrooms in butter. Add soup, milk, seafood, mustard, and cayenne. Spoon into 4 individual baking dishes; sprinkle with cheese and paprika. Bake at 400°F. for 15 minutes or until hot. 4 servings.

GRATIN OF OYSTERS AND SPINACH

2 tablespoons sliced green onion
1 tablespoon butter or margarine
1 can (10 fl. ounces) condensed
  oyster stew
1 soup can milk
2 slices bacon, cooked and crumbled
½ cup cooked chopped spinach
¼ cup shredded Swiss cheese

In saucepan, cook onion in butter until tender. Add remaining ingredients. Heat until cheese melts; stir now and then. 2 to 3 servings.

BARBECUE-BAKED FISH

1 pound fish fillets (thaw if frozen)
1 tablespoon butter or margarine
4 thin slices lemon
4 thin onion rings
2 tablespoons chopped parsley
1 can (10 fl. ounces) condensed
  tomato soup

In baking dish (10x6x2") place fish; sprinkle with salt, pepper. Dot with butter; top with lemon, onion, parsley. Bake at 350°F. for 15 minutes. Pour soup over, stirring in liquid around fish. Bake 10 minutes more or until done. Stir before serving. 3 servings.

DEVILED CRAB

1 can (10 fl. ounces) condensed
  cream of celery soup
1 cup flaked cooked crab, or 1 can
  (7 ounces), drained
2 tablespoons chopped green
  pepper
1 tablespoon chopped onion
2 teaspoons lemon juice
1 teaspoon Worcestershire
½ teaspoon prepared mustard
2 tablespoons buttered bread
  crumbs

Combine all ingredients, except bread crumbs; spoon into 4 small buttered baking dishes. (Clam shells are attractive for this.) Sprinkle crumbs over crab mixture. Bake in a 350° oven 20 minutes or until lightly browned. 2 to 3 servings.

OYSTERS À LA QUEEN

½ cup sliced mushrooms, drained
¼ cup chopped onion
2 tablespoons butter or margarine
2 tablespoons flour
1 can (10 fl. ounces) condensed
   oyster stew
¼ cup milk
2 tablespoons diced pimiento

In saucepan, brown mushrooms and cook onion in butter until tender. Blend in flour; gradually stir in stew, milk, and pimiento. Heat, stirring until thickened. Makes about 2 cups. Serve over cooked chicken, fish, broccoli spears, or asparagus spears.

CREAMED SALMON

¼ cup chopped onion
1 tablespoon butter or margarine
1 can (10 fl. ounces) condensed
   cream of mushroom or celery soup
⅓ to ½ cup milk
1 can (7¾ ounces) salmon, or 1 can
   (7 ounces) tuna, drained and
   flaked
¾ cup cooked green beans
1 tablespoon lemon juice (optional)

Cook onion in butter until tender. Blend in soup, milk, fish, green beans, and lemon juice. Heat; stir often. Serve over toast or rice. 2 to 3 servings.

SEAFOOD AU GRATIN

1 can (10 fl. ounces) condensed
   Cheddar cheese soup
¼ cup milk
2 cups cooked seafood (shrimp, lobster, crab, white fish, or any combination of these)
1 tablespoon chopped parsley
¼ cup buttered bread crumbs

In 1-quart casserole, stir soup until smooth; gradually add milk. Mix in seafood and parsley. Top with bread crumbs. Bake in a 400° oven 30 minutes or until bubbling. 3 to 4 servings.

SHRIMP WITH NOODLES

1 can (10 fl. ounces) condensed
   cream of mushroom soup
½ cup sour cream
¼ cup water
1½ cups diced cooked shrimp
⅛ teaspoon paprika
Cooked noodles

In saucepan, combine all ingredients except noodles. Heat; stir now and then. Serve over noodles. 4 servings.

Saucery

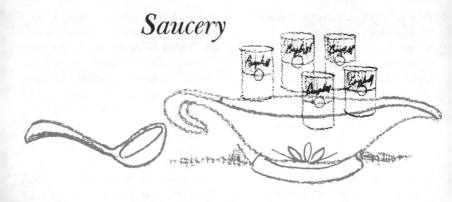

Lucky the housewife who discovers the versatile sauces always on hand in cans of condensed soup. Whether you're adding new flavour appeal to leftover meat or preparing gravy for a chicken, a can of soup is ready to fill your sauce-making needs with magical ease.

White sauce or cream sauce comes all blended for you in a can of cream soup. Whenever a recipe calls for white sauce, take a can of soup. Choose the one with the extra-special flavour you want—cream of chicken, mushroom, or celery soup. Simply add a little liquid to thin the soup sauce to the thickness you prefer, and use it as a pour-on cream sauce.

Gravy, also, is always available in the cream soups. Just blend with a little liquid and/or drippings for the kind of gravy menfolk applaud.

VERSATILE CREAM SAUCE

1 can (10 fl. ounces) condensed cream of celery, chicken, or mushroom soup
¼ to ½ cup milk

Pour soup into pan. Stir to blend. Add milk. Heat; stir often. Makes about 1½ cups sauce. Use for creaming vegetables and meats.

INSTANT CHEESE SAUCE: Pour 1 can Cheddar cheese soup into pan. Stir contents well to blend. Stir in ¼ to ⅓ cup milk. Heat slowly, stirring often.

4-WAY CHEESE SAUCE: Pour 1 can any cream soup into pan. Stir to blend. Add ¼ to ½ cup milk and ½ cup shredded Canadian Cheddar cheese. Heat; stir often.

SPECIAL QUICK SAUCES

Type Sauce	Use 1 can Soup	Add and Heat
Almond for chicken, veal, seafood	Cream of chicken or mushroom	⅓ cup water, ¼ cup chopped almonds, and 1 tablespoon minced onion browned in butter; 1 tablespoon sherry (optional)
Creamy Cheese for vegetables or chicken	Cream of celery	Blend 4-ounce package of softened cream cheese with soup before adding ¼ to ⅓ cup milk
Curry for chicken, veal, lamb, or seafood	Cream of asparagus, celery, or chicken	¼ to ⅓ cup milk and ¼ to 1 teaspoon curry powder
Herb for chicken, fish, veal, vegetables, eggs	Cream of celery, chicken, or mushroom	¼ to ½ cup milk and dash of basil, marjoram, poultry seasoning, sage, or thyme
Nut for chicken, veal, or vegetables	Cream of mushroom	⅓ to ½ cup milk and ¼ cup chopped walnuts or other nuts
Parsley for fish, eggs, vegetables	Cream of celery	¼ to ⅓ cup milk and 1 tablespoon chopped parsley
Pimiento-Egg for fish	Cream of celery	⅓ cup water, 1 tablespoon chopped onion browned in butter, 1 hard-cooked egg (chopped), 2 tablespoons chopped pimiento
Poulette for chicken or fish	Cream of chicken	¼ to ⅓ cup milk and 2 tablespoons minced onion browned in butter, 2 tablespoons chopped parsley, 2 teaspoons lemon juice, and 1 to 2 tablespoons sherry (optional)
Sour Cream for beef, chicken, fish	Cream of mushroom	¼ to ½ cup water, 2 tablespoons chopped onion browned in butter, ¼ cup sour cream, ⅛ teaspoon paprika

TOMATO SOUP SAUCE

Plain Sauce: Heat tomato soup just as it comes from the can. You may want to thin it a bit by adding a little water. Season as you like—with prepared mustard or horseradish, Worcestershire, "Tabasco" sauce, lemon juice, or herb such as thyme or oregano. 1¼ cups sauce. Use as a pour-on for: Pork chops, beef patties, corned beef hash, wieners, or fish sticks.

Tomato Horseradish Sauce: Stir in 2 tablespoons prepared horseradish, 1 tablespoon prepared mustard, dash of ground cloves, and pepper. 1½ cups sauce. Serve with beef, ham, wieners, or meat loaf.

Tomato Cheese Sauce: Add ⅓ cup milk and ½ cup shredded Canadian Cheddar cheese. Heat; stir often until cheese is melted. 1⅔ cups sauce. Serve with fish, omelet, or vegetables.

EGG CHEESE SAUCE

1 can (10 fl. ounces) condensed
   Cheddar cheese soup
¼ cup milk
1 hard-cooked egg, sliced
¼ teaspoon prepared mustard

Stir soup until smooth. Gradually blend in milk; add egg and mustard. Heat; stir often. 1½ cups sauce. Serve over cooked broccoli or cauliflower.

SAUCE CREVETTES

1 tablespoon chopped green onion
Dash crushed thyme leaves
1 tablespoon butter or margarine
1 can (10 fl. ounces) condensed
   cream of mushroom soup
½ cup milk
1 cup diced cooked shrimp
1 tablespoon chopped ripe olives

In saucepan, cook onion with thyme in butter until onion is tender. Add remaining ingredients. Heat; stir now and then. Serve over poached eggs on toast. Makes 2 cups sauce.

54

CREAMY TOMATO SAUCE

¼ cup chopped onion
⅛ teaspoon leaf thyme
1 tablespoon butter or margarine
1 can (10 fl. ounces) condensed
   tomato soup
½ cup sour cream
¼ cup water
2 teaspoons paprika
¼ teaspoon salt
Dash pepper

Cook onion and thyme in butter until onion is tender. Blend in remaining ingredients. Heat; stir often. Makes 2 cups sauce. Serve with chicken or veal.

SHRIMP-FISH SAUCE

¼ cup chopped cucumber
2 tablespoons chopped onion
2 tablespoons butter or margarine
1 can (10 fl. ounces) condensed
   cream of celery soup
⅓ cup milk
1 teaspoon lemon juice

In saucepan, cook onion in butter until tender. Add remaining ingredients. Heat; stir now and then. Makes about 2 cups. Serve over cooked shrimp or white fish.

HERB-CHEESE SAUCE

1 can (10 fl. ounces) condensed
   cream of mushroom soup
⅓ to ½ cup milk
1 cup shredded Canadian Cheddar
   cheese
1 tablespoon chopped parsley
Generous dash tarragon, crushed

Stir soup until smooth; blend in milk. Add remaining ingredients. Heat; stir often. 2 cups sauce. Serve over cooked peas and onions, green beans or broccoli.

STROGANOFF SAUCE

¼ cup chopped onion
½ teaspoon paprika
2 tablespoons butter or margarine
1 can (10 fl. ounces) condensed
   golden mushroom soup
¼ cup sour cream

In saucepan, cook onion with paprika in butter until tender. Stir in soup and sour cream. Heat; stir now and then. Makes 1½ cups sauce. Serve with beef patties or sliced cooked beef or veal.

SPAGHETTI WITH CLAM-OYSTER SAUCE

½ cup chopped onion
¼ cup chopped parsley
1 medium clove garlic, minced
2 tablespoons olive oil
1 can (10 fl. ounces) condensed
  oyster stew
2 cans (5 ounces each) minced
  clams, drained
1 teaspoon lemon juice
Cooked spaghetti

In saucepan, cook onion, parsley, and garlic in oil until onion is tender. Add stew, clams, and lemon juice. Heat; stir now and then. Serve over spaghetti. Makes about 2 cups sauce.

WHITE CLAM SAUCE

1 can (5 ounces) minced clams,
  drained
1 medium clove garlic, minced
2 tablespoons butter or margarine
1 can (10 fl. ounces) condensed
  cream of mushroom soup
½ cup water
2 tablespoons chopped parsley
½ pound spaghetti, cooked

In saucepan, cook clams and garlic in butter a few minutes. Stir in soup, water, and parsley. Heat; stir now and then. Serve over spaghetti. 4 servings.

CELERY-CAPER SAUCE FOR COLD MEAT

1 can (10 fl. ounces) condensed
   cream of celery soup
¼ cup mayonnaise
1 tablespoon capers

Place unopened can of soup in refrigerator 3 or 4 hours. Blend soup and mayonnaise; stir in capers. Serve with cold cooked salmon, sliced beef, or ham. 1½ cups sauce.

VARIATIONS:

Dill Sauce: Substitute 1 teaspoon lemon juice and ½ teaspoon dried dill leaves for capers. Serve with cold cooked salmon. 1½ cups sauce.

Horseradish Sauce: Substitute 1 to 2 teaspoons horseradish for capers. Serve with cold sliced beef or ham. 1½ cups sauce.

Mustard Sauce: Substitute 1 teaspoon mustard for capers. Serve with cold sliced beef or ham. 1½ cups sauce.

SAUCE A L'ORANGE

1 tablespoon chopped onion
2 tablespoons butter, margarine, or
   drippings
1 can (10 fl. ounces) condensed
   cream of mushroom soup
⅓ cup orange juice
1 teaspoon grated orange rind
⅛ teaspoon ground ginger

Brown onion in shortening. Blend in remaining ingredients; stir until smooth. Heat. 1½ cups sauce. Especially good with roast duck.

ZESTY TOMATO TOPPER FOR EGGS

¼ pound sausage links, thinly sliced
¼ cup chopped onion
2 tablespoons chopped green
   pepper
1 can (10 fl. ounces) condensed old
   fashioned tomato rice soup
½ cup water
1 tablespoon dry red wine
   (optional)

Cook sausage slices until lightly browned; pour off excess drippings. Add onion and green pepper; cook until tender. Blend in remaining ingredients. Cook over low heat 10 minutes; stir often. 4 servings. Serve over omelet or scrambled eggs.

ALMOND-CHEESE SAUCE

1 can (10 fl. ounces) condensed
   Cheddar cheese soup
¼ cup milk
¼ cup slivered almonds
¼ teaspoon curry powder

Stir soup until smooth. Gradually blend in milk; add remaining ingredients. Heat; stir often. 1½ cups sauce. Serve over cooked broccoli or cauliflower.

QUICK TOULONNAISE SAUCE

2 tablespoons sliced green onion
1 tablespoon butter or margarine
1 can (10 fl. ounces) condensed
  cream of celery soup
⅓ cup milk
2 tablespoons Chablis or other
  dry white wine
1 tablespoon capers
1 tablespoon chopped ripe olives

In saucepan, cook onion in butter until tender; add remaining ingredients. Heat; stir now and then. Makes 1½ cups sauce. Serve over asparagus.

TANGY FISH SAUCE

¼ cup chopped celery
1 small clove garlic, minced
⅛ teaspoon dry mustard
2 tablespoons butter or margarine
1 can (10 fl. ounces) condensed
  Cheddar cheese soup
⅓ cup milk
1 tablespoon chopped dill pickle

In saucepan, cook celery with garlic and mustard in butter until tender. Add remaining ingredients. Heat; stir now and then. Makes about 1½ cups. Serve over cooked white fish.

MOCK HOLLANDAISE

1 can (10 fl. ounces) condensed
  cream of celery, chicken, or
  mushroom soup
½ cup milk
2 tablespoons butter or margarine
2 tablespoons lemon juice
2 egg yolks, slightly beaten

Combine all ingredients. Heat over low heat just until thickened, stirring constantly. *Do not boil.* 1⅔ cups sauce. Serve with cooked vegetables or fish.

EASY HOLLANDAISE: Use any cream soup. Omit milk, butter, and egg yolks. Reduce lemon juice to 1 tablespoon and add ¼ cup mayonnaise.

SAUCE CREOLE

1 small green pepper, sliced
1 small onion, sliced
½ cup sliced mushrooms, drained
2 tablespoons butter or margarine
1 can (10 fl. ounces) condensed
  tomato soup
¼ cup water
1 teaspoon vinegar

Cook green pepper, onion, and mushrooms in butter until tender. Stir in remaining ingredients. Cook over low heat 5 minutes. 2 cups sauce. Serve over omelet, hamburgers, or baked fish.

SOUPER GRAVY

1 can (10 fl. ounces) condensed
   cream of celery, chicken, mushroom or golden mushroom soup
¼ to ⅓ cup water
2 to 4 tablespoons drippings or
   butter

When preparing gravy for roast or fried meat, remove meat from pan and pour off and measure drippings. Pour can of soup into pan; stir well to loosen browned bits. Blend in water and drippings for thickness desired. Heat; stir often. 1½ cups gravy. Serve with fried chicken, roast beef, roast pork, pork chops, hamburgers, or baked ham.

QUICK ONION GRAVY

1 cup sliced onion
1 small clove garlic, minced
3 tablespoons butter or margarine
1 can (10 fl. ounces) condensed
   golden mushroom soup
½ cup water

In saucepan, cook onion and garlic in butter until tender. Stir in soup and water. Heat; stir now and then. Serve over beef patties or sliced cooked beef or pork.

CREAMY GIBLET GRAVY

4 ounces chicken giblets, chopped
   and cooked
½ cup chopped celery
2 tablespoons butter or margarine
1 can (10 fl. ounces) condensed
   cream of chicken soup
⅓ cup water

Brown giblets and cook celery in butter until tender. Blend in remaining ingredients. Heat; stir often. 2 cups gravy.

Barbecue Bonanza

Catch a whiff of meat or poultry barbecuing! That's the call to good eating . . . for barbecues can be held inside (on a rotisserie, in the oven, on an hibachi in the fireplace, or even in a frying pan on top of the range), or outdoors on plain or fancy grills. Whatever the location it's smart to reach for the soup can for rare finds in easy, zesty sauces when the cook moves to preparation of a barbecue.

An easy reputation as a barbecue chef is yours with a good sauce, good brush (long-handled or pastry), and a cut of meat which turns crisp and luscious over carefully controlled heat. Select your recipe from the following pages.

ALL 'ROUND TOMATO BARBECUE SAUCE

1 can (10 fl. ounces) condensed
tomato soup
2 to 4 tablespoons sweet pickle
relish
¼ cup chopped onion
1 tablespoon brown sugar
1 tablespoon vinegar
1 tablespoon Worcestershire

Combine all ingredients. Cover; simmer until onion is cooked and flavours are blended. 1½ cups sauce.

BARBECUED WIENERS

ON TOP OF STOVE: Combine sauce as directed. Add 1 pound wieners. Cover; simmer 20 minutes; stir often. 4 to 5 servings.

OUTDOOR COOKING: Prepare sauce as directed. Slit 2 pounds wieners lengthwise; brush with sauce. Place on grill over glowing coals. Cook, brushing with sauce and turning every few minutes, until nicely browned. 4 to 5 servings.

BARBECUED HAMBURGERS

ON TOP OF STOVE: Shape 2 pounds seasoned ground beef into 8 patties. Brown in butter or margarine. Add sauce ingredients. Simmer until patties are done. 8 servings.

OUTDOOR COOKING: Prepare sauce as directed. Make patties as in top of stove method. Place on grill about 6 inches above glowing coals. Cook about 15 minutes, brushing with sauce and turning every 5 minutes. 8 servings.

BARBECUED CHICKEN

ON TOP OF STOVE: Brown 2 pounds chicken parts in 2 to 4 tablespoons butter or margarine. Add sauce ingredients. Cover; simmer 45 minutes or until chicken is done. Stir now and then. 4 to 6 servings.

OUTDOOR COOKING: Combine sauce ingredients. Divide 2 pounds chicken parts on sheets of double thickness heavy duty aluminum foil (about 2 or 3 pieces chicken per sheet). Spread with about ¼ cup of sauce. Fold foil over; bring edges together; seal tightly with double fold. Cook on grill 4 to 5 inches above bed of hot coals 40 to 45 minutes. Turn packets over now and then. 4 to 6 servings.

BARBECUED STEAK

OUTDOOR COOKING: Prepare sauce. Place steak (2 pounds, cut ¾-inch thick) on grill about 4 inches above glowing coals. Brush with sauce; cook 5 minutes. Turn; brush with sauce. Cook 5 minutes longer or until desired doneness. Heat remaining sauce. Serve with steak. 4 to 6 servings.

SAUCE FOR BARBECUE SANDWICHES

⅓ cup chopped green onion
1 tablespoon chopped hot cherry
  peppers
2 tablespoons butter or margarine
1 can (10 fl. ounces) condensed
  tomato soup
¼ cup water
1 tablespoon brown sugar
1 teaspoon prepared horseradish

Cook onion and peppers in butter until onion is tender. Add remaining ingredients. Simmer 15 minutes or until flavours are blended; stir often. 1⅓ cups sauce.

WIENER SANDWICHES

Prepare sauce. Slit 1 pound wieners lengthwise. Place on broiler pan; brush with sauce. Broil about 3 inches from heat until done, brushing with sauce and turning often. Serve on toasted buns. 4 to 5 servings.

BURGER SANDWICHES

Prepare sauce. Shape 1½ pounds seasoned ground beef into 6 patties. Place on broiler pan; brush with sauce. Broil about 3 inches from heat until done, brushing with sauce and turning often. Serve on toasted buns. 6 servings.

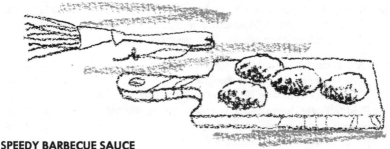

SPEEDY BARBECUE SAUCE

1 can (10 fl. ounces) condensed
  onion soup
½ cup ketchup
2 tablespoons salad oil
1 large clove garlic, minced
4 drops "Tabasco" sauce
¼ teaspoon salt
Dash pepper

Combine all ingredients. Cover; simmer 10 minutes; stir often. Makes 1½ cups sauce. Use sauce for basting hamburgers, wieners, chicken, or spareribs. Serve extra sauce over meats.

ONION BARBECUE SAUCE

1 can (10 fl. ounces) condensed
  cream of mushroom soup
1 can (10 fl. ounces) condensed
  onion soup
½ cup ketchup
¼ cup salad oil
¼ cup vinegar
2 large cloves garlic, minced
2 tablespoons brown sugar
1 tablespoon Worcestershire
⅛ teaspoon "Tabasco" sauce

Combine all ingredients. Cover; simmer 15 minutes; stir often. 3⅓ cups sauce. Use for chicken, ribs.

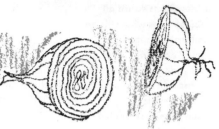

OUTDOOR CHICKEN

Prepare sauce. Brush 4 split broilers with salad oil. Place on grill (skin-side up) about 6 inches above glowing coals. Cook 15 minutes; turn; cook 15 minutes more. Brush with sauce; continue cooking 30 minutes or until chicken is done, brushing with sauce and turning every 5 minutes. 8 servings.

OUTDOOR SPARERIBS

Place 6 pounds spareribs (cut into serving-size pieces) in a large pot of boiling water. Cover; simmer 1 hour; drain. Prepare sauce as directed. Place ribs on grill about 6 inches above glowing coals. Brush with sauce; continue cooking 30 minutes or until done, brushing with sauce and turning every 5 minutes. 6 servings.

OVEN BARBECUED SPARERIBS

4 pounds spareribs, cut in serving-
  size pieces
1 can (10 fl. ounces) condensed
  beef broth
1½ cups mincemeat
3 tablespoons vinegar

Place spareribs in roasting pan (13 x 9 x 2"). Bake in a 350° oven 1 hour; pour off fat. Combine remaining ingredients; pour over ribs. Bake 1½ hours more or until done; baste now and then. 4 to 6 servings.

OUTDOOR CHICKEN OR SPARERIBS

Prepare sauce. Use 2 split broilers or 4 pounds spareribs. Follow cooking directions for outdoor chicken or spareribs in Onion Barbecue Sauce recipe. 4 servings.

BARBECUED LAMB KABOBS

1 can (10 fl. ounces) condensed
   tomato soup
1 small clove garlic, minced
2 tablespoons salad oil
2 tablespoons wine vinegar
1 tablespoon sugar
½ teaspoon salt
⅛ teaspoon pepper
⅛ teaspoon leaf oregano, crushed
Dash leaf thyme
1 pound lamb (from leg), cut in
   1½-inch cubes
1 medium green pepper, cut in
   1½-inch pieces
1 medium onion, cut in ½-inch slices

Blend soup, garlic, oil, vinegar, sugar, and seasonings. Add lamb; stir until well coated. Cover; place in refrigerator 4 hours. On 4 skewers arrange alternately lamb, green pepper, and onion. Place on broiler rack. Brush kabobs with sauce. Broil about 3 inches from heat for 30 minutes or until meat is tender. Brush kabobs with sauce and turn every 3 or 4 minutes. 4 servings.

NOTE: To cook outdoors: Prepare kabobs as directed above. Place on grill about 4 to 5 inches above glowing coals. Brush kabobs with sauce. Cook 25 to 30 minutes or until meat is tender, brushing with sauce and turning every few minutes. 4 servings.

TOP OF STOVE BARBECUED CHICKEN

2 pounds chicken parts
½ teaspoon salt
Dash pepper
¼ cup butter or margarine
1 can (10 fl. ounces) condensed
   tomato soup
½ cup chopped onion
3 tablespoons wine vinegar
2 tablespoons brown sugar
1 tablespoon Worcestershire
Dash sweet basil
Dash leaf thyme
5 drops "Tabasco" sauce

Season chicken with salt and pepper; brown in butter. Stir in remaining ingredients. Cover. Cook over low heat 45 minutes or until chicken is tender; stir now and then. 4 to 6 servings.

Vegetables with New Flavour

There are new ways to interest your family in vegetables! Reach for a can of soup.

Whether you cook a mixture of garden vegetables French style in clear consommé, or dish up a casserole of green beans baked to creamy perfection, your family will cheer these dishes they often otherwise neglect.

Here are the easiest ways in the world to cook flavourful creamed onions, add unexpected tang and colour to baked potatoes, prepare scalloped potatoes that will get rave requests for seconds. Try creaming all kinds of vegetables in soup.

VEGETABLE-CHEESE BAKE

1 large bunch broccoli or head cauliflower (or two 10-ounce packages frozen) cooked and drained

1 can (10 fl. ounces) condensed cream of celery, chicken, or mushroom soup

⅓ to ½ cup milk

½ cup shredded sharp Canadian Cheddar cheese

¼ cup buttered bread crumbs

Place broccoli or cauliflower in shallow baking dish (10 x 6 x 2″). Blend soup, milk, and cheese; pour over vegetable. Top with crumbs. Bake in a 350° oven 30 minutes or until bubbling. 6 servings.

EASY CREAMED VEGETABLES

Top of stove method: Cook 2 packages (10 or 12 ounces each) frozen vegetables (cauliflower, corn, green beans, lima beans, mixed vegetables, peas, peas and carrots, spinach) in unsalted water until tender; drain. Stir in 1 can condensed cream of celery, chicken, mushroom, or Cheddar cheese soup; heat. Thin to desired consistency with milk. Season to taste. 6 servings.

SAVOURY POTATOES

2 slices bacon
½ cup chopped onion
1 can (10 fl. ounces) condensed cream of mushroom soup
Dash pepper
⅓ cup milk
5 cups cubed cooked potatoes

In saucepan, cook bacon until crisp; remove and crumble. Pour off all but 2 tablespoons drippings. Cook onion in drippings until tender. Stir in soup and pepper; gradually blend in milk. Add potatoes. Heat; stir now and then. 6 to 8 servings.

SCALLOPED POTATOES

1 can (10 fl. ounces) condensed Cheddar cheese, cream of celery, chicken, or mushroom soup
½ cup milk
Dash pepper
4 cups thinly sliced potatoes
1 small onion, thinly sliced
1 tablespoon butter or margarine
Dash paprika

Blend soup, milk, and pepper. In buttered 1½-quart casserole, arrange alternate layers of potatoes, onion, and sauce. Dot top with butter; sprinkle with paprika. Cover; bake in a 375° oven 1 hour. Uncover; bake 15 minutes more. 4 to 6 servings. NOTE: Sliced cooked potatoes may be substituted for raw potatoes. Mince onion and reduce cooking time to about 30 minutes; bake uncovered.

CHINESE VEGETABLES

2 cups diagonally sliced celery
1 cup diagonally sliced green onion
2 tablespoons salad oil
1 can (10 fl. ounces) condensed beef broth
1 can (5 ounces) bamboo shoots, drained
1 can (19 ounces) bean sprouts, drained
1 can (5 ounces) water chestnuts, drained and sliced
2 tablespoons cornstarch
2 tablespoons soy sauce

In frying pan, cook celery and onion in oil until just tender. Add remaining ingredients except rice. Cook over low heat, stirring until sauce thickens. Serve over rice. Serve with additional soy sauce. 6 servings.

CREAMED ONIONS AND PEAS

1 can (10 fl. ounces) condensed
cream of chicken or mushroom
soup
⅓ cup milk
1 package (12 ounces) frozen peas,
cooked and drained
12 cooked small white onions,
drained
Dash pepper

Blend soup and milk; add peas, onion, and pepper. Heat; stir often. 4 to 6 servings.

NOTE: If desired, substitute 2 cups cubed cooked potatoes for onions. Decrease milk to ¼ cup.

VEGETABLES IN CHEESE SAUCE

2 packages (10 ounces each) frozen
broccoli or cauliflower, cooked
and drained
1 can (10 fl. ounces) condensed
Cheddar cheese soup
¼ cup milk
¼ cup buttered bread crumbs

Place broccoli in shallow baking dish (10 x 6 x 2"). Blend soup and milk; pour over broccoli. Top with crumbs. Bake in a 350° oven about 30 minutes or until hot and bubbling. 6 to 8 servings.

ONIONS AMANDINE

1 can (10 fl. ounces) condensed
cream of celery or mushroom soup
4 cups cooked small white onions
½ cup shredded Canadian Cheddar
cheese
¼ cup chopped toasted almonds

Stir soup until smooth; mix with onions in 1½-quart casserole. Sprinkle cheese and nuts on top. Bake in a 375° oven 30 minutes. 6 servings.

NOTE: If desired, substitute cashews, peanuts, or pecans for almonds.

ZESTY BEAN

2 tablespoons chopped onion
2 tablespoons chopped green pepper
1 tablespoon butter or margarine
1 can (10 fl. ounces) condensed tomato soup
¼ cup water
1 tablespoon brown sugar
1 tablespoon vinegar
1 teaspoon prepared mustard
2 cans (12 ounces) lima beans, drained

Brown onion and green pepper in butter. Add remaining ingredients except beans. Heat. Put beans in buttered 1-quart casserole; pour sauce over. Bake in a 375° oven 45 minutes. 4 to 6 servings.

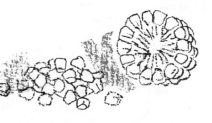

CREAMY CORN SCALLOP

1 can (10 fl. ounces) condensed cream of celery, chicken, or mushroom soup
1 tablespoon minced onion
Dash pepper
1 can (12 ounces) whole kernel corn, drained
1 cup crumbled soda crackers
2 tablespoons butter or margarine

Combine soup, onion, and pepper. In 1-quart casserole, arrange alternate layers of corn, soup mixture, and crackers; dot with butter. Bake in a 400° oven 25 minutes. 6 servings.

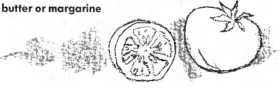

SUMMERTIME FRIED TOMATOES

4 medium tomatoes, sliced
⅓ cup seasoned flour
¼ cup butter or margarine
1 can (10 fl. ounces) condensed cream of mushroom soup
⅓ cup milk

Dip tomato slices in seasoned flour. Cook in butter over low heat until lightly browned on both sides. Remove to heated platter. Stir soup and milk into skillet. Heat. Pour sauce over tomatoes. 4 to 6 servings.

GLAZED CARROTS

2 tablespoons chopped onion
1 tablespoon chopped parsley
2 tablespoons butter or margarine
8 medium carrots, cut in 1-to
  1 ½-inch slices
1 can (10 fl. ounces) condensed
  consommé
Dash ground nutmeg

Cook onion and parsley in butter about 5 minutes. Add remaining ingredients. Cover; cook over medium heat 25 minutes. Uncover; continue cooking 20 minutes or until carrots are tender and sauce thickens and glazes carrots. (Watch carefully during last few minutes to prevent sticking.) 4 servings.

NOTE: To shorten cooking time, cut carrots in ½-inch slices. Cook, uncovered, about 30 minutes.

ITALIAN EGGPLANT BAKE

1 medium eggplant, peeled and cut
  in 1- to 1 ½-inch cubes
1 large onion, sliced
1 medium green pepper, sliced
½ small clove garlic, minced
1 teaspoon leaf oregano, crushed
¼ cup butter or margarine
1 can (10 fl. ounces) condensed
  tomato soup
1 cup water
¼ teaspoon salt
Garlic croûtons (see index)
Grated Parmesan cheese

Cook eggplant in boiling salted water for 3 minutes; drain and place in shallow baking dish (10 x 6 x 2"). Cook onion, green pepper, garlic, and oregano in butter until tender. Add soup, water, and salt. Heat; pour sauce over eggplant. Bake in a 350° oven 45 minutes; stir often. Remove eggplant from oven. Turn temperature up to 425°. Top eggplant with croûtons; sprinkle with cheese. Return to oven; bake 15 minutes more. 6 servings.

GREEN BEAN CASSEROLE

1 can (10 fl. ounces) condensed
  cream of chicken or mushroom
  soup
½ cup milk
1 teaspoon soy sauce
Dash pepper
3 cups cooked French style green
  beans (or two 10-ounce packages
  frozen)
1 can (6 ounces) French fried
  onions

In 1½-quart casserole, stir soup, milk, soy sauce, and pepper until smooth; mix in beans and ½ can onions. Bake at 350°F. for 25 minutes or until hot. Stir. Top with remaining onions. Bake 5 minutes more. 6 servings.

Egg and Cheese Cookery

Eggs and cheese enjoy a reputation of true versatility. Excellence and simplicity reign where soup and eggs or cheese are combined for meatless meals.

Soup sauces enrich egg dishes, help make cheese fondues and casseroles full of flavour. When it comes to a soufflé, you'll find you can make this "show-off" dish with any of 4 kinds of soup— and have the finest results. If it's a cheese sauce you need, look in the Saucery section.

Remember, both eggs and cheese are delicate . . . neither should be cooked at high temperatures.

EGG CROQUETTES

1 can (10 fl. ounces) condensed cream of celery, chicken, or mushroom soup
8 hard-cooked eggs, sieved or very finely chopped
¼ cup fine dry bread crumbs
2 tablespoons minced parsley
2 tablespoons minced onion
½ teaspoon salt
Dash pepper
2 tablespoons shortening
⅓ cup milk

Mix ¼ cup soup with eggs, bread crumbs, parsley, onion, and seasonings; form into 6 croquettes. (If mixture is difficult to handle, chill before shaping.) Roll in additional bread crumbs. Fry croquettes slowly in shortening until browned. Meanwhile, combine remaining soup with milk. Heat. Serve as sauce over croquettes. 3 servings.

EASY CHEESE SOUFFLÉ

1 can (10 fl. ounces) condensed
  Cheddar cheese soup
6 eggs, separated

Heat soup in saucepan, stirring; remove from heat. Beat egg yolks until thick and lemon-coloured; stir into soup. In large bowl, using clean egg beater, beat egg whites until stiff; fold soup mixture into egg whites. Pour into 1½-quart casserole. Bake in a 300° oven 1 to 1¼ hours or at 400° for 30 minutes. Serve immediately. 4 to 6 servings.

SOUPER CHEESE SOUFFLÉ

1 can (10 fl. ounces) condensed
  cream of celery, chicken, or
  mushroom soup
1 cup shredded sharp process
  cheese
6 eggs, separated

Combine soup and cheese; heat slowly until cheese melts. Beat egg yolks until thick and lemon-coloured; stir into soup mixture. Beat egg whites until stiff; fold soup mixture into egg whites. Pour into ungreased 2-quart casserole. Bake in a 300° oven 1 to 1¼ hours, or in a 400° oven 30 minutes. Serve immediately. 4 to 6 servings.

Try these additions to vary the basic soufflé:

Shrimp Surprise Soufflé: ½ cup minced cooked broccoli, well drained, ¼ teaspoon lemon juice, and a dash ground nutmeg to cream of shrimp soup-cheese mixture. Proceed as above.

Asparagus Soufflé: ⅛ teaspoon ground nutmeg and ½ cup chopped cooked asparagus to cream of mushroom soup-cheese mixture. Proceed as above.

Ham-Mushroom Soufflé: ¼ teaspoon chervil, ½ cup finely minced cooked ham, and 2 tablespoons chopped parsley to cream of mushroom soup-cheese mixture. Proceed as above.

RUM TUM DITTY

1 can (10 fl. ounces) condensed
  tomato soup
¼ cup water
1 cup shredded sharp Canadian
  Cheddar cheese
3 to 4 slices toast

Combine soup, water, and cheese. Cook over low heat; stir often until cheese is melted. Serve over toast. 3 to 4 servings. If desired, garnish with hard-cooked egg slices or sardines.

EASY EGGS BENEDICT

1 can (10 fl. ounces) condensed
   cream of celery, chicken, or
   mushroom soup
⅓ cup milk
6 thin slices ham, fried
6 slices buttered toast or English
   muffin halves
6 eggs, poached
1 tablespoon minced parsley

Blend soup and milk. Heat. Meanwhile, place a slice of ham on each slice of toast or muffin half; top with poached egg. Pour sauce over eggs. Sprinkle with minced parsley. 6 servings.

SHRIMP OMELET

SAUCE:
1 can (10 fl. ounces) condensed
   cream of mushroom soup
1 cup diced cooked shrimp
⅓ cup milk
2 tablespoons chopped parsley

OMELET:
8 eggs
½ cup milk
¼ teaspoon salt
Dash pepper
4 tablespoons butter or margarine

To make sauce, in saucepan, combine soup, shrimp, milk, and parsley. Heat; stir now and then. To make omelet, beat eggs, milk, salt, and pepper. In frying pan, melt butter; pour in egg mixture. Cook slowly. As undersurface becomes set, lift slightly to allow uncooked egg to flow underneath and cook. When omelet is done, transfer to platter. Make a shallow cut down the centre; pour part of sauce on half of the omelet; fold over. Serve with remaining sauce. 4 servings.

STRACCIATELLE

1 can (10 fl. ounces) condensed
   chicken with rice soup
1 soup can water
1 egg
2 tablespoons grated Parmesan
   cheese
1 tablespoon chopped parsley

In saucepan, combine soup and water. Heat. Beat egg with cheese and parsley; gradually pour into simmering soup, stirring gently until egg is set. Serve immediately. 2 to 3 servings.

CREAMED EGGS

1 can (10 fl. ounces) condensed Cheddar cheese or cream of celery soup
⅓ to ½ cup milk
4 hard-cooked eggs, sliced
2 tablespoons chopped pimiento
4 slices toast

Blend soup and milk. Add eggs and pimiento. Heat; stir often. Serve on toast. 4 servings.

EGGS GOLDENROD: Omit pimiento. Separate cooked egg yolks and whites; chop whites coarsely; force yolks through a fine sieve. Add egg whites to heated sauce. Garnish each serving with sieved yolk.

BAKED CHEESE FONDUE

3 eggs, separated
1 can (10 fl. ounces) condensed cream of celery, chicken, or mushroom soup
1 cup shredded sharp Canadian Cheddar or process cheese
¼ teaspoon dry mustard
2 cups small bread cubes

Beat egg whites until stiff but not dry. Beat egg yolks until thick. Blend in soup, cheese, and mustard; stir in bread cubes. Fold in egg whites. Spoon into 1½-quart casserole. Bake in a 325° oven 1 hour. 4 to 6 servings.

SWISS FONDUE

1 large clove garlic, cut in half
1 cup Chablis or other dry white wine
1 can (10 fl. ounces) condensed Cheddar cheese soup
1 pound natural Swiss cheese, cubed or shredded
3 tablespoons cornstarch
French or Italian bread cubes

Rub inside of fondue pot or saucepan with cut edge of garlic, then discard. In fondue pot, simmer wine. Blend in soup. Combine cheese and cornstarch; stir into soup mixture. Heat until cheese melts; stir now and then. Spear bread with fondue fork and dip into fondue. Makes about 4 cups.

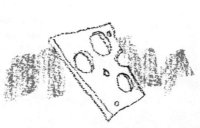

EGG AND OYSTERS AU GRATIN

1 can (10 fl. ounces) condensed
   oyster stew
¼ cup milk
2 tablespoons flour
½ cup shredded sharp Canadian
   Cheddar cheese
6 hard-cooked eggs, sliced
Cooked asparagus or broccoli spears

Empty stew into saucepan. Gradually blend milk into flour until smooth; slowly stir into stew. Add cheese. Cook, stirring until thickened and cheese is melted. Add eggs; heat. Serve over asparagus; garnish with paprika. 3 servings.

EGGS FLORENTINE

2 cups chopped cooked spinach (or
   two 12-ounce packages frozen),
   drained
6 eggs
1 can (10 fl. ounces) condensed
   cream of celery or mushroom soup
1 cup shredded mild process cheese

Cover bottom of shallow baking dish (10 x 6 x 2") with cooked spinach; break eggs and place on top. Pour soup around eggs completely covering spinach; sprinkle with cheese. Bake in a 350° oven 25 to 30 minutes or until eggs are done. 6 servings.

QUICK EGG CURRY

1 can (10 fl. ounces) condensed
   cream of mushroom soup
⅓ cup milk
1 teaspoon curry powder
4 hard-cooked eggs, sliced
4 slices bread, toasted
Shredded coconut, toasted slivered
   almonds, chutney, or raisins

Stir soup until smooth. Blend in milk and curry powder. Heat; stir often. Add eggs. Serve over toast with coconut, almonds, chutney, or raisins. 4 servings.

WESTERN SCRAMBLE

½ cup chopped cooked ham
¼ cup chopped green pepper
¼ cup chopped onion
4 tablespoons butter or margarine
1 can (10 fl. ounces) condensed
   Cheddar cheese soup
8 eggs, slightly beaten

In 10-inch frying pan, brown ham and cook green pepper and onion in butter until tender. Meanwhile, in bowl, stir soup until smooth; gradually blend in eggs. Add to ham mixture. Cook over low heat; do not stir. As mixture begins to set around edges, gently lift cooked portions with large turner so that thin, uncooked portion can flow to the bottom. Continue gently lifting cooked portions until eggs are completely set, but still moist (about 8 minutes). 4 servings.

Instant Cheese Sauce Page 52

EGGS IN CHEESE SAUCE

1 can (10 fl. ounces) condensed
  cream of celery or mushroom soup
⅓ to ½ cup milk
½ cup shredded sharp Canadian
  Cheddar cheese
4 hard-cooked eggs, sliced
4 slices toast
Chopped parsley, if desired

Combine soup, milk, and cheese. Cook over low heat until cheese melts. Stir often. Add eggs. Serve on toast, rice, or asparagus. Garnish with parsley. 4 servings.

CURRIED EGGS

6 hard-cooked eggs
¼ cup mayonnaise
¼ teaspoon curry powder
1 can (10 fl. ounces) condensed
  cream of mushroom soup
½ cup milk
Toast or English Muffins, split and
  toasted
Paprika

Cut eggs in half lengthwise. Carefully remove egg yolks. In small bowl, mash yolks with fork. Blend in mayonnaise and curry powder. Stuff into egg whites. In pan, combine soup and milk. Arrange eggs filled side up in sauce. Cover; cook over low heat 5 minutes or until eggs are hot. Serve eggs on toast; spoon sauce over all. Sprinkle with paprika. 3 servings.

GOLDEN RABBIT

1 can (10 fl. ounces) condensed
  Cheddar cheese soup
1 can (10 fl. ounces) condensed
  tomato soup
¼ cup milk
6 slices toast or crackers

Stir cheese soup until smooth. Gradually blend in tomato soup and milk. Heat; stir often. Serve over toast or crackers. 4 to 6 servings.

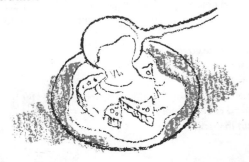

Baked Stuffed Tomatoes Page 99

Salads and Salad Dressings

Do you yearn for a special blend of seasonings to give your salads a special lift? Does your husband admire a hearty potato salad of robust flavour? Are you looking for a colourful molded salad to serve at luncheon; for smooth yet not-too-rich dressings, to set off a bowl of greens? You'll find your answer here; each flavoured with that secret ingredient, a can of condensed soup.

HAM AND MACARONI TOSS

1 can (10 fl. ounces) condensed
  cream of chicken soup
¼ cup chopped celery
¼ cup chopped onion
2 tablespoons chopped green
  pepper
½ teaspoon prepared mustard
Dash "Tabasco" sauce
Dash pepper
2 cups cooked macaroni
1½ cups diced cooked ham
Tomatoes, cut in wedges

Combine soup, celery, onion, green pepper, mustard, "Tabasco" sauce, and pepper. Add macaroni and ham. Chill. Serve with tomato wedges. 4 servings.

TIP: To unmold gelatin salads, dip pan bottom briefly in warm (not hot) water. Run knife along edges to permit air to flow in. Tap sharply once or twice. Invert on moistened serving plate (this permits you to shift mold if necessary); raise pan and release salad.

SEASHORE SALAD

2 envelopes unflavoured gelatin
2 cups cold water
1 can (10 fl. ounces) condensed tomato soup
1 tablespoon lemon juice
1 package (8 ounces) cream cheese, softened
1 cup diced cooked shrimp
½ cup chopped celery
2 tablespoons chopped green onion

In saucepan, sprinkle gelatin on cold water to soften. Place over low heat, stirring until gelatin is dissolved. Remove from heat; gradually stir in soup and lemon juice. Stir cream cheese until smooth; gradually blend in gelatin mixture. Chill until slightly thickened. Fold in remaining ingredients. Pour into 1-quart mold. Chill until firm. Unmold and serve on crisp salad greens. Makes about 4 cups.

CREAMY TUNA MOLD

2 envelopes unflavoured gelatin
2 cups cold water
1 can (10 fl. ounces) condensed cream of celery soup
1 tablespoon lemon juice
1 package (4 ounces) cream cheese, softened
1 can (7 ounces) tuna, drained and flaked
½ cup shredded carrot
½ cup chopped celery
2 tablespoons chopped parsley

In saucepan, sprinkle gelatin on 1 cup cold water to soften. Place over low heat, stirring until gelatin is dissolved. Remove from heat. Blend soup and lemon juice into cream cheese; gradually blend in gelatin and remaining water. Chill until slightly thickened. Fold in remaining ingredients. Pour into 5-cup mold. Chill until firm. Unmold; serve on crisp salad greens. Makes about 4½ cups.

ROSY AND WHITE ASPIC

1 envelope unflavoured gelatin
½ cup cold water
1 can (10 fl. ounces) condensed tomato soup
1 teaspoon grated onion
Crisp salad greens
1 cup creamy cottage cheese

Sprinkle gelatin on cold water to soften. Place over low heat; stir until gelatin is dissolved. Remove from heat; combine with soup and onion. Pour into 1-quart or 4 individual molds that have been rinsed with cold water. Chill until firm. Unmold; serve on salad greens with a topping of cottage cheese. Makes about 4 cups.

DOUBLE DECKER CHICKEN MOLD

First layer:
1 **envelope unflavoured gelatin**
½ **cup cold water**
1 **can (10 fl. ounces) condensed cream of chicken soup**
¼ **cup mayonnaise**
1 **tablespoon lemon juice**
1 **can (6 ounces) boned chicken, or 1 cup diced cooked chicken**
¼ **cup chopped celery**
2 **tablespoons chopped toasted almonds**
1 **tablespoon finely chopped onion**
Dash pepper

First layer: Sprinkle gelatin on cold water to soften. Place over low heat; stir until gelatin is dissolved. Remove from heat. Blend soup, mayonnaise, and lemon juice; stir in gelatin . Chill until mixture begins to thicken. Fold in remaining ingredients. Pour into 1½-quart mold. Chill until almost firm.

Second layer:
1 **envelope unflavoured gelatin**
½ **cup water**
1 **can (14 ounces) jellied cranberry sauce**
1 **orange, peeled and diced**

Second layer: Sprinkle gelatin on cold water to soften. Place over low heat; stir until gelatin is dissolved. Remove from heat. Crush cranberry sauce with fork; add gelatin . Chill until mixture begins to thicken; fold in orange. Pour on top of chicken layer. Chill until firm. Unmold. Serve on crisp salad greens. Makes about 5 cups.

SPRINGTIME SALAD

1 **can (10 fl. ounces) condensed beef broth**
1 **package (3 ounces) lemon flavoured gelatin**
½ **cup cold water**
1 **tablespoon grated onion**
1 **tablespoon vinegar**
Dash salt
Dash pepper
1 **cup diced cooked beef**
⅓ **cup diced red apple**
2 **tablespoons sliced celery**

In saucepan, bring beef broth to a boil. Add gelatin ; stir to dissolve. Add water, onion, vinegar, salt, and pepper. Chill until slightly thickened. Fold in remaining ingredients. Pour into a 3-cup mold. Chill until firm (about 4 hours). Makes about 2½ cups.

GERMAN POTATO SALAD

4 slices bacon
¾ cup chopped onion
1 can (10 fl. ounces) condensed
  cream of celery or chicken soup
¼ cup water
2 to 3 tablespoons vinegar
½ teaspoon sugar
⅛ teaspoon pepper
4 cups sliced cooked potatoes
¼ cup chopped parsley

Cook bacon until crisp; remove from frying pan; drain and crumble. Cook onion in bacon drippings until tender. Blend in soup, water, vinegar, sugar, and pepper. Heat; stir now and then. Add potatoes, parsley, and bacon; simmer 5 minutes. Serve hot. 6 servings.

TOMATO FRENCH DRESSING

1 can (10 fl. ounces) condensed
  tomato soup
¼ cup vinegar
½ cup salad oil
1 tablespoon minced onion
2 tablespoons sugar
2 teaspoons dry mustard
1 teaspoon salt
¼ teaspoon pepper

Combine all ingredients in 1-quart jar. Shake well before using. About 2¼ cups.

NOTE: To vary this TOMATO FRENCH DRESSING, add any one of the following:

Bacon Dressing—4 slices bacon, cooked and crumbled
Blue Cheese Dressing—¼ cup crumbled blue cheese
Chiffonade Dressing—1 chopped hard-cooked egg, 1 tablespoon minced green pepper, 1 tablespoon minced pimiento
Curry Dressing—½ teaspoon curry powder
Garlic Dressing—1 clove garlic, minced
Herb Dressing—1 teaspoon ground herb (marjoram, rosemary, sage, savoury, or thyme)
Ripe Olive Dressing—¼ cup chopped ripe olives
Sweet Pickle Relish Dressing—¼ cup sweet pickle relish
Vinaigrette Dressing—1 chopped hard-cooked egg and 1 tablespoon chopped parsley

RUSSIAN-STYLE DRESSING

1 can (10 fl. ounces) condensed
   cream of celery soup
¼ cup mayonnaise
¼ cup chili sauce
1 teaspoon lemon juice
2 to 3 teaspoons minced onion,
   if desired

Place unopened can of soup in refrigerator 3 to 4 hours. Blend soup and mayonnaise; stir in remaining ingredients. Serve with asparagus or green salads. About 1¾ cups dressing.

QUICK GREEN GODDESS DRESSING

1 can (10 fl. ounces) condensed
   cream of celery soup
¼ cup mayonnaise
2 tablespoons chopped parsley
4 anchovies, chopped
1 teaspoon lemon juice

Place unopened can of soup in refrigerator 3 to 4 hours. Blend soup and mayonnaise; stir in remaining ingredients. Serve with green salads. About 1½ cups dressing.

DRESSING LAMAZE

1 can (10 fl. ounces) condensed
   tomato soup
1 cup mayonnaise
¼ cup India or sweet pickle relish
1 hard-cooked egg, chopped
½ teaspoon grated onion
½ teaspoon prepared mustard
1 tablespoon lemon juice

Blend soup and mayonnaise. Add remaining ingredients; mix well. Chill. Serve with cooked shrimp or green salads. About 2½ cups dressing.

LOW-CAL TOMATO DRESSING

1 can (10 fl. ounces) condensed
   tomato soup
¼ cup water
2 tablespoons lemon juice
2 teaspoons grated onion
½ teaspoon prepared mustard
¼ teaspoon salt
Generous dash pepper

Combine all ingredients in a tightly covered container; shake until blended. Chill 4 hours.

DIETERS' DELIGHT

1 can (10 fl. ounces) condensed
   beef broth
2 tablespoons chili sauce or ketchup
2 tablespoons vinegar
1 tablespoon grated onion
1 ounce crumbled blue cheese, if
   desired

Combine all ingredients. Shake well and serve over green salads. About 1¼ cups dressing.

Quick Breads and Pancakes

If you're looking for something new that's quick to get ready, with family-satisfying flavour, here's the formula: Prepare a stack of pancakes, or bake a quick bread (a mix does fine). Combine a creamy soup with chicken or ham or any of the combinations in recipes given here. Spoon the mixture over the hot bread, and you have a dish to do you proud.

Try a quick spoon bread with extra flavour baked right in the batter—soup does it!

MINUTE TURKEY SHORTCAKE

1 can (10 fl. ounces) condensed
  cream of chicken soup
½ cup milk
1½ cups diced cooked turkey
½ cup cooked peas
1 tablespoon chopped pimiento
4 biscuits, split

Blend soup and milk. Combine remaining ingredients except biscuits. Heat; stir often. Serve over biscuits. 4 servings.

SPOONBREAD

1 cup corn meal
1¼ cups water
3 tablespoons butter or margarine
1 can (10 fl. ounces) condensed
  Cheddar cheese, cream of chicken,
  or mushroom soup
1 teaspoon baking powder
3 eggs, separated

In saucepan, combine corn meal and water; bring to a boil and cook until very thick, stirring constantly. Remove from heat and stir in butter. Add soup, baking powder, and slightly beaten egg yolk; mix well. Fold mixture into stiffly beaten egg whites. Pour into greased 2-quart casserole dish. Bake at 350°F. for 1 hour. Serve hot with butter and maple syrup if desired. 6 servings.

CREAMED CHICKEN WITH ALMONDS OVER PANCAKES

1 cup chopped celery
2 tablespoons butter or margarine
1 can (10 fl. ounces) condensed
    cream of chicken or mushroom
    soup
⅓ to ½ cup milk
1 can (6 ounces) boned chicken, or
    1 cup diced cooked chicken
2 tablespoons diced pimiento
¼ cup toasted slivered almonds
8 thin pancakes

Cook celery in butter until tender; blend in soup and milk. Add chicken, pimiento, and almonds. Heat; stir often. Serve over pancakes. 3 to 4 servings.

HAM-AND-MUSHROOM-STUFFED PANCAKES

8 thin pancakes (about 7 inches in
    diameter)
¼ cup mushroom stems
    and pieces, drained and chopped
2 tablespoons finely chopped onion
2 tablespoons butter or margarine
8 thin slices boiled ham
1 can (10 fl. ounces) condensed
    cream of celery soup
½ cup sour cream
⅓ cup water
Paprika or chopped parsley

Prepare pancakes. In saucepan, cook mushrooms and onion in butter until onion is tender. Place a slice of ham and 2 teaspoons mushroom mixture on each pancake; roll. Keep warm in oven. Meanwhile, combine soup, sour cream, and water. Heat; stir now and then. Serve sauce over pancakes. Garnish with paprika or chopped parsley. 4 servings.

CHINESE SHRIMP PANCAKES

8 thin pancakes
3 tablespoons thinly sliced green
    onion
2 tablespoons butter or margarine
1 can (10 fl. ounces) condensed
    cream of chicken soup
1½ cups diced cooked shrimp
¼ cup sliced water chestnuts
¼ teaspoon soy sauce
¼ cup milk
¼ teaspoon Worcestershire
Dash hot pepper sauce

Prepare pancakes; keep warm. To make filling, in saucepan, cook green onion in butter until tender. Stir in ½ cup soup, shrimp, water chestnuts, and soy sauce. Heat; stir now and then. To make sauce, combine remaining soup, milk, Worcestershire, and hot pepper sauce. Heat; stir now and then. Place about ¼ cup filling on each pancake; roll up. Serve sauce over pancakes. 4 servings.

Surprise Cakes and Cookies

Tomato soup gives a wonder-what-it-is flavour and rosy colour to cakes and cookies.

Once tried, these are the unusual cake specialties you will want to make again and again. Some women win blue ribbons at fairs with tomato soup cakes; others bake them for holiday gifts. Most women make them just for the pleasure of baking an easy cake with fascinating flavour—a little spicy, a little tangy, and altogether special.

Like the convenience of cake mixes? You can make a delicious, moist cake by adding a can of tomato soup and two eggs to a package of spice cake mix.

Or surprise everyone by giving a subtle new taste to those time-honoured favourites, fruit cake and gingerbread. Tomato soup adds a distinctive flavour that'll have the family clamoring for more.

OLD FASHIONED GINGERBREAD CAKE

2 cans (10 fl. ounces each) condensed tomato soup

3 eggs

2 packages (about 13 ounces each) gingerbread mix

1 cup raisins

1 cup chopped walnuts

In large bowl or mixer, blend soup and eggs. Add gingerbread mix. Blend at low speed until thoroughly moistened; beat 2 minutes on medium speed. Fold in raisins and walnuts. Pour into well-greased 9-inch tube pan. Bake at 325°F. for 1 hour 15 minutes or until cake is done. Cool right side up in pan 10 minutes; then remove from pan. Serve warm or cool. Sprinkle top with icing sugar. Makes 9-inch tube cake.

GLAZE FOR OLD FASHIONED GINGERBREAD CAKE

1 cup sifted icing sugar
2 tablespoons rum
1 tablespoon melted butter

Combine all ingredients; beat until smooth. Makes enough glaze for a 9-inch tube cake.

TOMATO SOUP CAKE

2 ¼ cups cake flour or 2 cups all-purpose flour
1⅓ cups sugar
4 teaspoons baking powder
1 teaspoon baking soda
1 ½ teaspoons allspice
1 teaspoon cinnamon
½ teaspoon ground cloves
1 can (10 fl. ounces) condensed tomato soup
½ cup hydrogenated shortening
2 eggs
¼ cup water

Preheat oven to 350°F. Generously grease and flour two round layer pans. 8 or 9" or an oblong pan, 13x9x2". Measure dry ingredients into large bowl. Add soup and shortening. Beat at low to medium speed for 2 minutes (300 strokes with a spoon) scraping sides and bottom of bowl constantly. Add eggs and water. Beat 2 minutes more, scraping bowl frequently. Pour into pans. Bake 35 to 40 minutes. Let stand in pans 10 minutes; remove and cool on rack. Frost with Cream Cheese Frosting or favourite white frosting.

VARIATIONS: For a 9-inch tube pan. Prepare as above; bake 1 hour.
Nut or Raisin: After mixing, fold in 1 cup chopped nuts or 1 cup raisins. Bake 35 to 40 minutes.
Date and Nut: After mixing, fold in 1 cup chopped walnuts and 1 cup chopped dates. (Use 1 to 2 tablespoons flour to sprinkle over dates while chopping them.) Bake in 9" layers or 13 x 9 x 2" pan for 40 to 45 minutes.

CREAM CHEESE FROSTING

Blend 2 packages (4 ounces each) cream cheese (softened) with 1 tablespoon milk. Gradually add 1 package (1 pound) sifted icing sugar; blend well. Mix in ½ teaspoon vanilla extract, if desired.

QUICK TOMATO SPICE CAKE

1 package (2 layer) spice cake mix
1 can (10 fl. ounces) condensed tomato soup
½ cup water
2 eggs

Mix *only* above ingredients; following directions on package. If desired, fold in 1 cup chopped walnuts. Bake as directed. Frost with Cream Cheese Frosting or other favourite white frosting.

EASY FRUIT CAKE

Prepare QUICK TOMATO SPICE CAKE. After mixing, fold in 1 cup chopped candied fruit and 1 cup chopped walnuts. Bake as directed on package adding about 5 minutes more.

FOR MINCEMEAT CAKE. Substitute ½ cup prepared mincemeat for candied fruit in EASY FRUIT CAKE. Bake in 9" layers or 13 x 9 x 2" pan.

PEACH OR PRUNE UPSIDE DOWN CAKE

Divide between two 9-inch round layer pans: ½ cup melted butter, ½ cup brown sugar; top with an arrangement of 1 can (1 pound) peach halves, drained, and ½ cup walnut pieces. Prepare QUICK TOMATO SPICE CAKE. Pour into pans spreading evenly over topping. Bake at 350°F. for 35 minutes. Run spatula around edge of pan. Immediately turn upside down on serving plate. Leave pan over cake 5 minutes. Serve warm or cooled.

FOR PRUNE CAKE: Follow directions above, substituting 1 can (1 pound) canned pitted prunes, drained.

FOAMY SAUCE
(For Steamed Pudding)

1 egg, separated
¾ cup icing sugar
¾ cup heavy cream, whipped
½ teaspoon vanilla extract

In small bowl of electric mixer, beat egg white until soft peaks form; *gradually* beat in sugar. Stir in egg yolk; fold in whipped cream and vanilla. Makes 2 cups.

STEAMED PUDDING

2½ cups sifted all-purpose flour
3 teaspoons baking powder
½ teaspoon baking soda
1 teaspoon ground cinnamon
½ teaspoon ground nutmeg
2 cups chopped dates or figs
¼ cup shortening
1 cup sugar
1 egg
1 can (10 fl. ounces) condensed tomato soup

Sift flour with baking powder, soda, and spices; dust dates or figs with small amount of flour mixture. Cream shortening and sugar; add egg and mix well. Add dry ingredients alternately with soup; stir well after each addition. Fold in dates or figs. Pour into greased 1½-quart mold; cover securely with aluminum foil. Place on trivet in large kettle. Add boiling water to one-half height of mold. Cover; steam 2 hours. Remove mold from water; uncover and loosen edges of pudding with knife. Unmold while hot; serve with one of the following sauces, Foamy Sauce or Hard Sauce.

HARD SAUCE

⅓ cup soft butter
1 cup sifted icing sugar
½ teaspoon vanilla extract

In bowl, soften butter. Add sugar, a little at a time; beat until creamy and smooth. Stir in vanilla extract. Chill until hard. ¾ cup sauce.

ROSY ROCKS

1½ cups all-purpose flour
1⅓ cups sugar
1 teaspoon baking powder
½ teaspoon baking soda
2 teaspoons cinnamon
1 teaspoon allspice
1 cup shortening
1 egg
1 can (10 fl. ounces) condensed tomato soup
2 cups uncooked rolled oats
1 cup seedless raisins
1 cup chopped walnuts

Preheat oven to 350°F. Sift dry ingredients except oats together into large bowl. Add shortening, egg, and soup. Beat at medium speed for 2 minutes. (300 strokes with a spoon), scraping sides and bottom of bowl constantly. Stir in oats, raisins, and nuts. Drop rounded teaspoonfuls on ungreased cookie sheet. Bake about 15 minutes or until lightly browned. Makes about 7 dozen cookies.

Party and International Specialties

"Let's have a party."

Happy words indeed. And they lead up to some of the most memorable occasions for every family—when good friends get together.

What kind of party? Name most any kind—and good food will be a key factor to its success: Children's birthdays. Teenage record hops. Grandparents' golden wedding anniversary. Even when the girl next door comes for coffee, it can be a party.

TODAY'S SERVICE, BUFFET STYLE

An easy style of service is a major requirement for today's parties because of smaller homes without dining rooms and little outside help. Buffet service is the answer for many a hostess. Nothing is more dazzling for guests to behold than a buffet table covered with colourful tempting foods. Each one picks up a plate and helps himself while the hostess guides the proceedings.

Successful buffets are those where guests are at ease to enjoy the company and the food. Some pointers to follow are these:

1. Plan the menu with an eye for colour. If the main dish is a casserole, top it with golden cheese or some slices of tomato or stuffed olives for that bit of colour.
2. Serve at least one hot dish (perhaps a vegetable). Or if you're serving mainly hot foods, include relishes or a chilled fruit dessert for contrast.
3. Plan the food so the main course and accompaniments can all go on one's dinner plate. To achieve this, it's often helpful to serve vegetable relishes and spiced fruits instead of a salad.
4. Fork foods are best because guests won't have to worry about several pieces of silverware to juggle. Plan a meat that can be cut with a fork (for example—sliced ham or boned chicken); or use a main dish such as chicken à la king which requires no cutting.
5. Trays are a necessity if guests do not sit at a table to eat.

GOOD STARTERS

The appetizer course starts a party in sparkling fashion. This is why it's becoming fashionable to serve a "cup of soup" in the living room for guests to sip and savour before the meal. Now's the time to bring forth your handsome old tureen or a lovely pitcher for a pouring soup.

Select the soup course from any of those given in the "Appetizer Soup" section. Or perhaps one of these:

FRISKY SOUR

2 cans (10 fl. ounces each) condensed beef broth
½ soup can water
8 ice cubes
¼ to ⅓ cup lemon juice

Put all ingredients in a shaker or jar with tight fitting cover. Cover and shake well. Serve in chilled glasses. 4 to 6 servings.

FLAMING BEAN SOUP

2 cans (10 fl. ounces each) condensed bean with bacon soup
1 can (10 fl. ounces) condensed beef broth
2 soup cans water
¼ cup sherry or bourbon
Lemon slices

Blend soups; add water. Heat; stir often. Pour into heat-proof chafing dish or tureen. To flame, heat the sherry or bourbon in a ladle. Put a lighted match to warmed liquor. While flaming, lower into the soup. Stir to blend the flavours before ladling out this warming brew. Pass lemon slices for garnish. 6 servings.

TANGY PEA BOWL

¼ cup canned sliced mushrooms, drained
⅛ teaspoon thyme
1 tablespoon butter or margarine
1 can (10 fl. ounces) condensed green pea soup
1 soup can water

Lightly brown mushrooms with thyme in butter. Add soup; gradually stir in water. Heat; stir often. 2 to 3 servings.

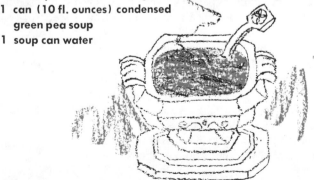

PARTY PATTERN SOUPS

Often just a small touch of decoration for food can give a party air to a simple menu—which may be merely soup and sandwiches. For example, an easy-to-do soup garnish can be croûtons cut in various shapes to make "Party Pattern Soups".

BRIDGE LUNCHEON: Cut white bread into bridge shapes (diamonds, hearts, clubs, and spades)—use small cookie cutters. Toast lightly and float the croûton on each bowl of cream soup.

Other party-pattern garnishes to try:
- Valentine's Day: Heart-shaped croûtons.
- St. Patrick's Day: Shamrock-shaped croûtons.
- July First: Maple Leaf shaped croûtons.
- Halloween: Pumpkin-shaped croûtons.
- Christmas: Simple tree-shaped croûtons.

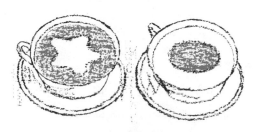

SPECIALTY DISHES

"Make one great dish your specialty" is a secret to successful parties used by many a hostess. You can borrow from the great cooking of the world to make dishes with that gourmet flair. Many ideas follow.

WHEN THE GALS MEET

Chilled "V-8"   Sesame Seed Wafers
Seafood Curry*
Mixed Green Salad
Pineapple Parfait   Fancy Cookies
Tea or Coffee

PAELLA

2 pounds chicken parts
2 tablespoons salad oil
1 can (10 fl. ounces) condensed
    beef broth
2 medium cloves garlic, minced
2/3 cup raw regular rice
1/2 cup chopped canned tomatoes
1/2 cup chopped green pepper
2 tablespoons chopped pimiento

In frying pan, brown chicken in oil; pour off fat. Add broth and garlic. Cover; cook over low heat 15 minutes. Stir remaining ingredients into broth. Cover; cook 30 minutes more or until liquid is absorbed. Stir now and then. 4 servings.

SEAFOOD CURRY

1/4 cup chopped onion
1 teaspoon curry powder
1 tablespoon butter or margarine
1 can (10 fl. ounces) condensed
    cream of celery soup
1/3 cup milk
1 cup diced cooked shrimp
1/2 cup flaked cooked crab meat
Cooked rice or patty shells

In saucepan, cook onion with curry in butter until tender. Add soup, milk, shrimp, and crab. Heat; stir now and then. Serve over rice. 4 servings.

JAMBALAYA

1 cup ham cut in strips
1 cup chopped onion
1/2 cup green pepper cut in squares
1 medium clove garlic, minced
2 tablespoons salad oil
1 can (10 fl. ounces) condensed
    tomato soup
2 cups water
2/3 cup raw rice
1 medium bay leaf
Dash "Tabasco" sauce
1 cup cooked shrimp
Chopped parsley

In large frying pan, brown ham and cook onion, green pepper, and garlic in oil until vegetables are tender. Add remaining ingredients except shrimp and parsley. Bring to a boil. Cover; cook over low heat 20 minutes. Stir now and then. Stir in shrimp; cook 5 minutes more or until rice is tender. Garnish with parsley. 4 servings.

A TOUCH OF PARIS

French Onion Soup* (see index)
Scallops Parisienne*
Buttered Green Peas
Endive Salad with Tomato French Dressing*
French Bread   Butter
Fruit Turnovers (from freezer)
Coffee

SCALLOPS PARISIENNE

1 pound fresh scallops
½ cup canned sliced mushrooms,
    drained
2 tablespoons chopped onion
2 tablespoons butter or margarine
1 can (10 fl. ounces) condensed
    Cheddar cheese soup
2 teaspoons lemon juice
Dash pepper
Dash crushed thyme leaves
Dash ground marjoram
2 tablespoons buttered bread
    crumbs
Paprika

In saucepan, cook scallops in water over low heat for 10 minutes; drain well. Divide among 4 individual baking dishes. Meanwhile, in saucepan, brown mushrooms and cook onion in butter until tender. Add soup, lemon juice, and seasonings; pour over scallops. Top with crumbs; sprinkle with paprika. Bake at 350°F. for 30 minutes or until hot. 4 servings.

PILAF

½ cup fine egg noodles, broken
    in pieces
2 tablespoons butter or margarine
1 can (10 fl. ounces) condensed
    beef broth
⅓ cup water
½ cup raw regular rice

In saucepan, brown noodles in butter; stir often. Add remaining ingredients. Bring to a boil; stir. Cover; cook over low heat 20 to 25 minutes or until liquid is absorbed. 3 to 4 servings.

ARTICHOKE CASSEROLE

½ cup canned sliced mushrooms, drained
1 tablespoon butter or margarine
1 can (10 fl. ounces) condensed Cheddar cheese soup
½ cup milk
2 tablespoons sherry
1 ½ cups cooked rice
1 jar (6 ounces) artichoke hearts, cooked and drained
Paprika

In saucepan, brown mushrooms in butter; add soup, milk, and sherry. In 1-quart casserole, combine soup mixture, rice, and artichokes. Bake at 350°F. for 30 minutes; stir. Sprinkle with paprika. 4 to 6 servings.

SUPPER ITALIANO

Antipasto Tray
Chicken Cacciatore with Spaghetti*
Romaine Salad
Bread Sticks
Fruit   Cheese
Café Espresso

CHICKEN CACCIATORE

2 pounds chicken parts
2 tablespoons shortening
1 can (10 fl. ounces) condensed tomato soup
¼ cup dry red wine or 1 tablespoon vinegar
½ cup chopped onion
2 large cloves garlic, minced
½ teaspoon oregano, crushed
⅛ teaspoon salt
½ medium green pepper, cut into strips

In frying pan, brown chicken in shortening; pour off fat. Add remaining ingredients except pepper. Cover; cook over low heat 30 minutes; stir now and then. Add pepper; cook 15 minutes more. 4 servings. Serve with spaghetti.

IT'S A CURRY PARTY
Supper Party Starter*
Curried Chicken with Almonds*
Parsley Rice   Chutney
Jellied Vegetable Salad
Coconut Cake   Ice Cream
Coffee

CURRIED CHICKEN WITH ALMONDS

1 pound chicken breasts
3 tablespoons seasoned flour
Shortening
1 can (10 fl. ounces) condensed
  cream of chicken soup
½ to ¾ cup water
½ to 1 teaspoon curry powder
¼ cup toasted slivered almonds

Dust chicken with seasoned flour. Brown chicken in shortening. Combine remaining ingredients except almonds; pour over chicken. Cover. Cook over low heat 40 minutes or until chicken is tender. Stir often. (Add a little more water if necessary.) Add almonds. Cover. Cook 5 minutes more. 2 to 3 servings.

CHICKEN PAPRIKA

4 pounds chicken parts
⅓ cup seasoned flour
⅓ cup shortening
2 cans (10 fl. ounces each)
  condensed tomato soup
½ cup water
1 cup canned sliced mushrooms,
  drained
½ cup chopped onion
1 tablespoon paprika
1 large bay leaf
1 cup sour cream

Dust chicken with flour; brown in shortening in large frying pan. Pour off fat. Stir in remaining ingredients except sour cream. Cover; simmer 45 minutes or until tender. Stir now and then. Remove bay leaf. Blend in sour cream. Heat. Serve with noodles. 8 servings.

SOUPER MACARONI AND CHEESE

The favourite basic casserole to go with any meat dish at your buffet supper.

3 cups cooked macaroni
1 tablespoon butter or margarine
1 can (10 fl. ounces) condensed
  cream of mushroom soup
⅓ cup water
2 cups shredded Canadian Cheddar
  cheese
1 tablespoon finely minced onion

In 1½-quart casserole, blend hot cooked macaroni with butter. Stir in soup, water, 1½ cups cheese, and onion. Sprinkle remaining cheese on top. Bake in a 350° oven about 30 minutes or until browned and bubbly. 4 servings.

TOMATO MACARONI: Use ingredients and directions as above, but substitute 1 can condensed tomato soup for the cream of mushroom soup.

BREAST OF CHICKEN MAGNIFIQUE

4 whole chicken breasts (about 3 pounds), split
¼ cup butter or margarine
2 cups sliced mushrooms (about ½ pound)
2 cans (10 fl. ounces each) condensed cream of chicken soup
1 large clove garlic, minced
Generous dash crushed thyme
⅛ teaspoon rosemary, crushed
⅔ cup light cream

Use 1 large frying pan or prepare in 2 frying pans (10 inch) by dividing the ingredients equally. Brown chicken in butter; remove. Brown mushrooms. Stir in soup, garlic, and seasonings; add chicken. Cover; cook over low heat 45 minutes. Stir now and then. Blend in cream; heat slowly. Serve with rice. 8 servings.

CHICKEN VIA VENETO

4 pounds chicken parts
¼ cup flour
¼ cup butter
1 cup ham strips
2 cans (10 fl. ounces each) condensed Cheddar cheese soup
1 cup chopped canned tomatoes
3 medium onions, quartered
1 teaspoon basil, crushed

Use 1 large frying pan or prepare in 2 frying pans (about 10 inch) by dividing ingredients equally. Dust chicken with flour; brown in butter; remove. Brown ham. Stir in soup, tomatoes, onions, and basil; add chicken. Cover; cook over low heat 45 minutes or until tender. Stir now and then. Uncover; cook until desired consistency. 8 servings.

CHINESE HOT POT

2 chicken breasts (about 1½ pounds), split, skinned, and boned
2 packages (10 ounces each) frozen cut asparagus
½ pound thinly sliced mushrooms (about 2 cups)
8 cups cleaned fresh spinach (about 10 ounces)
2 cans (10 fl. ounces each) condensed chicken with rice soup
2 soup cans water
Soy sauce

Cut chicken into thin strips. On serving platter, arrange chicken, asparagus, mushrooms, and spinach. Prepare at table in 10-inch oven frying pan over direct heat or an electric frying pan. Combine soup and water; heat to boiling. Add half of the chicken, asparagus, and mushrooms; cook over low heat 3 minutes. Add half of the spinach; cook 2 minutes more or until just done. Remove with slotted spoon and serve with soy. Meanwhile, cook remaining chicken and vegetables as above. Heat broth; serve in soup bowls, if desired. 4 servings.

NEAR EAST MEATBALLS

1 pound ground beef
¼ cup fine dry bread crumbs
2 tablespoons milk
¼ teaspoon salt
½ cup canned sliced mushrooms, drained
1 tablespoon shortening
1 can (10 fl. ounces) condensed onion soup
1 cup water
½ cup uncooked rice
Minced parsley

Combine ground beef, bread crumbs, milk, and salt. Shape into 18 meatballs. Brown meatballs and mushrooms in shortening. Pour in soup and water; bring to a boil; stir in rice. Cover; simmer gently 30 minutes or until rice is tender. Stir often. Garnish with parsley. 4 servings.

QUICK LASAGNE

½ cup ground beef
1 cup chopped onion
2 large cloves garlic, minced
2 teaspoons oregano, crushed
2 cans (10 fl. ounces each) condensed tomato soup
½ cup water
2 teaspoons vinegar
½ pound plain lasagne noodles, cooked and drained
1 pint cottage cheese or ricotta
½ pound Mozzarella cheese, thinly sliced
Grated Parmesan cheese

In saucepan, brown beef and cook onion, garlic, oregano. Add soup, water, vinegar. Simmer 30 minutes; stir now and then. In baking dish (12 x 8 x 2″), arrange 3 alternate layers of noodles, cottage cheese, meat sauce, Mozzarella. Top with Parmesan. Bake at 350°F. for 30 minutes. Let stand 15 minutes. 6 servings.

MOCK SUKIYAKI

1 pound round steak, cut in very thin strips
2 tablespoons salad oil
1 can (10 fl. ounces) condensed beef broth
1½ cups sliced celery
1 medium green pepper, cut in strips
1 large onion, thinly sliced
1½ cups sliced fresh mushrooms
½ cup green onion cut in 1-inch pieces
1 tablespoon soy sauce
¼ cup water
2 tablespoons cornstarch

In large frying pan, brown steak in oil. Add broth, vegetables, and soy. Cover; cook over low heat about 10 minutes or until tender. Stir now and then. Combine water and cornstarch; stir into meat mixture. Cook, stirring until thickened. Serve over rice. 4 servings.

DAD'S BIRTHDAY DINNER

Pork Chops with Party Hats*
Scalloped Potatoes* (see index)   Brussels Sprouts
Apple and Nut Salad   Muffins
Birthday Cake
Coffee   Milk

PORK CHOPS WITH PARTY HATS

6 pork chops (about 1 ½ pounds)
Salt and pepper
6 onion slices
6 green pepper rings
1 can (10 fl. ounces) condensed tomato soup

In oven-proof frying pan, brown chops; pour off fat. Season with salt and pepper. Place slice of onion and pepper ring on each; pour soup over. Cover; bake at 350°F. for 1 hour or until chops are tender. 4 servings.

VEAL SWISS STYLE

1 ½ pounds thinly sliced veal cutlet
3 slices (3 ounces) Swiss cheese, cut in half
3 slices (3 ounces) boiled ham, cut in half
4 tablespoons butter or margarine
1 can (10 fl. ounces) condensed cream of mushroom soup
¼ teaspoon paprika
½ cup milk
¼ cup sauterne or other dry white wine

Cut veal into 12 oblong pieces; pound with meat hammer. On each of 6 pieces place ½ slice cheese and ham; top with remaining veal. Fasten securely with toothpicks. In large frying pan, brown veal in butter. Stir in remaining ingredients. Cook over low heat 30 minutes or until tender; stir now and then. 6 servings.

VEAL MARSALA

1 pound veal, thinly sliced
¼ cup grated Parmesan cheese
2 tablespoons flour
Dash pepper
½ cup canned sliced mushrooms, drained
¼ cup butter or margarine
1 can (10 fl. ounces) condensed beef broth
2 tablespoons Marsala or dry red wine (optional)
Cooked noodles or spaghetti

Cut veal into 2- or 3-inch pieces. Mix cheese, flour, and pepper; pound into veal with meat hammer or edge of heavy saucer. Brown veal, then mushrooms, in butter. Blend in any remaining flour and cheese. Add beef broth and wine. Cover. Cook over low heat 30 minutes or until meat is tender; stir often. Uncover; cook until sauce is desired consistency. Serve over noodles or spaghetti. 4 servings.

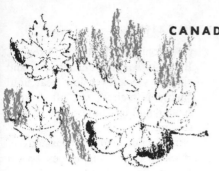

CANADIAN—ALL THE WAY

Cream of Mushroom Soup
Saucy Sirloin*
Hot Rice   Green Beans Amandine
Assorted Relishes
Brown 'n Serve Rolls   Butter
Apple Strudel (from freezer)
Coffee

SAUCY SIRLOIN

1 ½ pounds sirloin steak, cut in thin
strips
2 tablespoons salad oil
1 can (10 fl. ounces) condensed
consommé
¼ cup Burgundy or other dry red
wine
½ cup diagonally sliced green
onion (1-inch pieces)
½ cup canned sliced mushrooms,
drained
1 teaspoon Worcestershire
Dash dry mustard

In frying pan, brown steak in oil; pour off fat. Add remaining ingredients. Cover; cook over low heat 20 minutes or until meat is tender. Stir now and then. Mix ¼ cup water and 2 tablespoons cornstarch; gradually blend into sauce. Cook, stirring until thickened. Serve over rice. 6 servings.

BAKED STUFFED TOMATOES

6 medium tomatoes
2 slices bacon
¼ cup chopped green pepper
¼ cup chopped onion
1 cup cooked corn
Generous dash pepper
¾ cup toasted buttered bread cubes
1 can (10 fl. ounces) condensed
cream of celery soup
¼ cup milk

Cut slice from top of tomatoes; scoop out and save pulp leaving ¼-inch shell. In frying pan, cook bacon; remove and crumble. Cook green pepper and onion in drippings until tender; stir in corn, pepper, and all but ½ cup tomato pulp. Cook over low heat 5 minutes. Place 1 tablespoon bread in each tomato; fill with vegetable mixture. Top with remaining bread. Place in baking dish; add water to just cover bottom of dish. Bake at 350°F. for 20 minutes. Meanwhile in saucepan, combine soup, reserved tomato pulp, milk, and bacon; heat but do not boil. Serve over tomatoes. 6 servings.

PARTY TETRAZZINI

2 tablespoons chopped onion
1 tablespoon butter or margarine
1 can (10 fl. ounces) condensed
  cream of mushroom soup
½ cup water
½ cup shredded sharp process
  cheese
1 tablespoon sherry (optional)
2 cups cooked spaghetti
1 cup diced cooked chicken
  or turkey
2 tablespoons chopped pimiento
1 tablespoon chopped parsley

Cook onion in butter until tender. Blend in soup, water, cheese, and sherry. Cook over low heat until cheese is melted; stir often. Add remaining ingredients; heat. 2 to 3 servings.

NOTE: For variety, instead of chicken in above recipe, brown 1 cup finely diced cooked ham along with onion; then prepare as directed.

GLAZED COLD MEATS

Have you ever wanted to set out a platter of cold meat for a crowd and then been disappointed to see how quickly they dry and curl? Try this simple attractive and delicious way to glaze a mixed platter of cold cuts, so that they may be arranged in advance.

1 envelope unflavoured gelatin
¼ cup cold water
1 can (10 fl. ounces) condensed
  consommé
1 teaspoon Worcestershire
2 teaspoons lemon juice
1 can (14 ounces) pitted cherries,
  drained and rinsed in cold water
Sliced cooked ham, beef, pork,
  or lamb

Sprinkle gelatin on cold water to soften. Place over low heat; stir until gelatin is dissolved. Add consommé, Worcestershire, lemon juice, and cherries. Chill until mixture begins to thicken. Meanwhile, arrange cold meats attractively on a platter. Spoon a thin layer of the cherry consommé over meat, arranging cherries down sides and center of platter. Chill until serving time.

PARTY SALADS

A spectacular gelatin salad, shaped in a handsome mold, is a happy choice for the *pièce de résistance* for your luncheon party in the summer.

Try this menu pattern—with endless variations—to please "the girls".

FAVOURITE SALAD LUNCHEON

Rumaki
Hawaiian Chicken Velvet Salad
Asparagus Spears   Hot Rolls
Sherbet   Angel Food Cake
Coffee or Tea

HAWAIIAN CHICKEN VELVET SALAD

1 envelope unflavoured gelatin
¼ cup cold water
1 can (10 fl. ounces) condensed
    cream of chicken soup
4 ounces cream cheese, softened
2 tablespoons lemon juice
Dash ground ginger
1 cup diced cooked chicken
½ cup drained pineapple tidbits
¼ cup chopped celery
¼ cup chopped green pepper
Crisp salad greens
Toasted slivered almonds

Sprinkle gelatin on cold water to soften. Place over low heat; stir until gelatin is dissolved. Remove from heat. Gradually blend soup into cream cheese; stir in gelatin, lemon juice, and ginger; add chicken, pineapple, celery, and green pepper. Pour into a 1-quart mold; chill until firm. Unmold; serve on crisp salad greens; garnish with toasted almonds. Makes about 4 cups.

BEEF TOMATO SALAD

2 envelopes unflavoured gelatin
1½ cups water
1 bay leaf
1 can (10 fl. ounces) condensed
    consommé
1 can (10 fl. ounces) condensed
    tomato soup
2 tablespoons vinegar
⅛ teaspoon celery salt
1 cup finely chopped cooked beef
½ cup chopped celery
¼ cup chopped cucumber
2 tablespoons chopped onion

In saucepan, sprinkle gelatin on water to soften. Add bay leaf. Place over low heat and stir until gelatin is dissolved. Remove from heat and stir in soups, vinegar, and celery salt. Remove bay leaf. Chill until mixture begins to thicken. Fold in remaining ingredients. Pour into 5½-cup mold. Chill until firm. Unmold; serve on crisp salad greens. Makes about 5 cups.

Special Occasion Meats

BEEF ITALIANO

1 boneless chuck (about 3 ½ pounds)
1 cup sliced onion
1 large clove garlic, minced
2 teaspoons oregano, crushed
1 can (10 fl. ounces) condensed tomato soup
½ cup water
Generous dash pepper

Trim fat from meat; place in roasting pan. Bake at 350°F. for 1 hour. Spoon off fat. Combine remaining ingredients; pour over meat. Cover; bake 2 hours more or until tender. Thicken sauce if desired. 6 servings.

STEWED CHICKEN WITH DUMPLINGS

2 pounds chicken parts
1 can (10 fl. ounces) condensed cream of chicken soup
1 cup water
4 small carrots, cut in 2-inch pieces
2 large stalks celery, cut in 2-inch pieces
1 medium onion, thinly sliced
Dash pepper
1 cup packaged biscuit mix
⅓ cup milk

Put chicken, soup, water, vegetables, and pepper in large heavy pot. Cover; simmer 40 minutes or until chicken is tender. Combine biscuit mix and milk; stir lightly with a fork. Drop dough by spoonfuls onto pieces of chicken. Cook, uncovered, 10 minutes. Cover; cook 10 minutes more. 4 servings.

ROSY HAM LOAF-HORSERADISH SAUCE

1 can (10 fl. ounces) condensed tomato soup
1 pound ground lean ham
½ pound ground lean pork
½ cup fine dry bread crumbs
⅓ cup minced onion
¼ cup finely chopped celery
1 egg, slightly beaten
½ teaspoon dry mustard
Dash pepper
2 teaspoons prepared horseradish

Measure ½ cup soup; mix *thoroughly* with ham, pork, crumbs, onion, celery, egg, mustard, and pepper. Shape *firmly* into loaf; place in shallow baking pan. Bake in a 350° oven about 1¼ hours. For sauce, blend remaining soup with horseradish; heat. Serve over loaf. 6 servings.

CREAMY VEAL

1 ½ pounds thinly sliced veal, cut in serving-size pieces
1 medium onion, sliced
1 clove garlic, minced
2 tablespoons butter or margarine
1 can (10 fl. ounces) condensed cream of mushroom soup
¼ cup water
2 teaspoons lemon juice
1 tablespoon Marsala
½ teaspoon paprika
Dash pepper
1 tablespoon chopped pimiento

Pound veal with meat hammer or edge of heavy saucer. In frying pan, brown veal and cook onion with garlic in butter until tender. Stir in soup, water, lemon juice, wine, paprika, and pepper. Cover; cook over low heat for 15 minutes or until tender. Stir now and then. Garnish with pimiento. 6 servings.

PORK GOULASH WITH NOODLES

¼ cup flour
½ teaspoon garlic salt
Dash pepper
1 ½ pounds lean pork cubes
2 tablespoons shortening
1 can (10 fl. ounces) condensed onion soup
½ cup water
1 cup cooked tomatoes
½ medium green pepper, cut into strips
¼ cup chopped celery
⅛ teaspoon ground thyme
2 cups cooked noodles (about 4 ounces uncooked)

Combine flour, garlic salt, and pepper; roll meat in this mixture. In frying pan, brown meat in shortening; pour off any excess drippings. Add soup, water, tomatoes, green pepper, celery, and thyme. Sprinkle remaining flour over mixture. Cover; simmer 1 hour or until meat is tender; stir often. Uncover; cook 15 minutes more to thicken sauce. Serve over noodles. 6 servings.

MARDI GRAS CHICKEN LIVERS

½ pound chicken livers
½ cup thinly sliced onion
⅓ cup thinly sliced celery
2 tablespoons butter or margarine
1 can (10 fl. ounces) condensed tomato soup
¼ cup chopped parsley
¼ cup water
¼ teaspoon lemon juice
Cooked rice

Cook livers, onion, and celery in butter in covered frying pan until tender. Add soup, parsley, water, and lemon juice. Heat; stir now and then. Serve on rice. 3 to 4 servings.

Cooking for a Crowd

Every so often you're called on to cook for a crowd—perhaps for a church supper or a P.T.A. fund raising.

It's easy to come up with large-scale dishes and serve them with ease if you plan on cook-ahead foods readily prepared in quantity. Soup makes an ideal first course, served from mugs or plates. Soup can contribute behind the scenes, too, in making "seconds—please" main dishes and tasty vegetables to serve a crowd happily, as in these recipes designed for 16 or 20 or more portions.

FLEET'S-IN CHOWDER

2 cups water
1½ teaspoons leaf thyme
¼ teaspoon garlic powder
3 medium bay leaves
8 cans (10 fl. ounces each) condensed clam chowder Manhattan style
6 soup cans water
2 cups flaked cooked white fish
¼ cup chopped parsley

Combine 2 cups water, thyme, garlic, and bay leaves. Cover; simmer 20 minutes; remove bay leaves. Add remaining ingredients. Heat; stir now and then. 20 servings, 1 cup each.

HARVEST SOUP

3 cans (10 fl. ounces each) condensed cream of chicken soup
3 cans (10 fl. ounces each) condensed tomato soup
8 soup cans water
3 cans (10 fl. ounces each) condensed chicken gumbo soup

Combine cream of chicken soup and tomato soup; stir until smooth. Blend in water and chicken gumbo soup. Heat. 20 servings, 1 cup each.

CLUB COCKTAIL

6 cans (10 fl. ounces each)
  condensed tomato soup
5 cans (10 fl. ounces each)
  condensed beef broth
5 soup cans cold water
2 teaspoons Worcestershire
Dash "Tabasco" sauce

Place cans of soup in refrigerator 3 to 4 hours to chill. Blend soups and water; stir in Worcestershire and "Tabasco" sauce. Serve in chilled bowls or cups. 20 servings. 1 cup each.

FAR EASTERN CHICKEN POT

8 cans (10 fl. ounces each) condensed cream of chicken soup
8 soup cans milk
¾ cup finely chopped blanched
  almonds
2 tablespoons chopped parsley
⅛ teaspoon ground cloves
¼ teaspoon ground nutmeg
6 drops "Tabasco" sauce

Blend soup and milk until smooth; add remaining ingredients. Heat; *do not boil.* 20 servings, 1 cup each.

FAVOURITE BEAN SOUP

7 cans (10 fl. ounces each)
  condensed bean with bacon soup
7 soup cans water
2 cans (19 ounces each) tomatoes
2 cups cooked lima beans, drained
2 tablespoons Worcestershire

Blend soup and water. Add remaining ingredients; cook over low heat 20 minutes. 20 servings, 1 cup each.

CHICKEN À LA KING

½ cup diced green pepper
¼ cup butter or margarine
6 cans (10 fl. ounces each)
  condensed cream of chicken soup
2 to 3 cups milk
1½ quarts diced cooked chicken
¼ cup chopped pimiento
⅛ teaspoon pepper
Toast or patty shells

In large pan, cook green pepper in butter until tender. Gradually blend in soup and milk; stir until smooth. Add chicken, pimiento, and pepper. Heat slowly; stir now and then. Serve on toast or in patty shells. 20 servings. (2/3 cup/serving).

PARTY-SIZE GREEN BEAN CASSEROLE

3 cans (10 fl. ounces each) condensed cream of mushroom soup
½ cup milk
1 tablespoon soy sauce
¼ teaspoon pepper
9 cups cooked French style green beans (or six 10-ounce packages frozen)
2 cans (6 ounces each) French fried onions

Combine soup, milk, soy sauce, and pepper; stir until smooth. Mix in beans, 1 can onions. Spoon into two 1½-quart casseroles. Bake in a 350° oven 30 minutes or until bubbling. Top with remaining onions. Bake 5 minutes more. 20 servings, ½ cup each.

BAKED TUNA 'N NOODLES

2 cups thinly sliced celery
½ cup chopped onion
¼ cup shortening
6 cans (10 fl. ounces each) condensed cream of celery or mushroom soup
3 cups milk
6 cups cooked medium noodles
6 cans (7 ounces each) tuna, drained and flaked
½ cup diced pimiento
½ cup buttered bread crumbs

Cook celery and onion in shortening until tender. Blend in soup and milk. Add remaining ingredients, except bread crumbs. Pour into four 1½-quart casseroles or 5 shallow baking dishes (10 x 6 x 2″). Sprinkle crumbs on top. Bake in a 375° oven 30 minutes or until bubbling and brown. 20 servings, 1 cup each. *Chicken 'N Noodles:* Substitute 6 cups diced cooked chicken for tuna. Use either cream of chicken or mushroom soup.

STUFFED TURKEY

6 slices bacon
1 cup sliced celery
½ cup chopped onion
1 package (8½ ounces) herb-
seasoned stuffing mix
2 cups coarse cornbread crumbs
1 can (10 fl. ounces) condensed
beef broth
1 egg, slightly beaten
10-pound turkey
1 can (10 fl. ounces) condensed
cream of mushroom soup
½ cup whole berry cranberry sauce
¼ cup orange juice

In frying pan, cook bacon until crisp; remove and crumble. Pour off all but 2 tablespoons drippings. Cook celery and onion in drippings until tender. Toss lightly with stuffing mix, cornbread, broth, and egg. Fill cavity of turkey loosely with stuffing. Truss; place in roasting pan. Cover with foil. Roast at 325°F. for about 4 hours (25 minutes per pound or until tender). Uncover last hour to brown. Remove turkey to serving platter. Skim fat from drippings; add remaining ingredients. Heat; stir to loosen browned bits. 12 servings.

CHICKEN SUPREME

10 pounds chicken parts (40
pieces) without wings and backs
1 cup seasoned flour
½ cup butter or margarine,
melted
6 cans (10 fl. ounces each)
condensed cream of chicken or
mushroom soup
1 cup water

Dust chicken with seasoned flour. Arrange pieces skin side down in 2 buttered baking pans (12 x 18 x 2″). Do not overlap. Dribble melted butter over chicken. Bake in a 400° oven 20 minutes. Turn chicken; bake 20 minutes longer. Blend soup and water; spread over chicken. Bake 20 minutes more or until tender. 20 servings.

BEEF ROULADES

4 pounds thinly sliced
round steak
4 cups prepared packaged
herb-seasoned stuffing
¼ cup shortening
2 cans (10 fl. ounces each) condensed cream of mushroom soup
1 cup water

Cut steak into 16 long pieces; pound with meat hammer or edge of heavy saucer. Place ¼ cup stuffing on each piece of steak; roll up; fasten with toothpicks. In large frying pan, brown in shortening; pour off fat. Stir in soup, water. Cover; simmer 1½ hours or until tender. Stir now and then. Uncover; cook until desired consistency. 16 servings.

Teen Soups and Snacks

Fun and good food go together when teens take over the kitchen.

Soups are favourites, hot and cold, in mugs, jugs, and bowls. Add quick hot sandwiches (fast and flavourful with soup seasoning), grilled snacks, cookies—a party is set before you know it!

You'll find menus and recipes here to add to your party fun. Browse through other chapters for make-your-own party menus, from Great Soups to a Tomato Soup Cake that's "in".

AFTER-SKATING WARM-UP

Mugs of Chickety Chick*
Cheese and Crackers
Apples   Oatmeal Cookies

CHICKETY CHICK

1 can (10 fl. ounces) condensed
   cream of chicken soup
1 soup can water
¼ teaspoon poultry seasoning

Combine all ingredients. Heat; stir often. Sip from heavy cups or mugs. 2 to 3 servings.

VACATION SPECIAL

Watch your P's and Q's while school's out.

1 can (10 fl. ounces) condensed
   tomato soup
1 soup can water
¼ cup cooked alphabet macaroni

Blend soup and water; add macaroni. Heat. 2 to 3 servings. Or for an easy switch, sprinkle alphabet cereal atop plain tomato soup.

CHILI BEEF WIENERS

¼ pound ground beef
1 can (10 fl. ounces) condensed
    beef with vegetables and barley
    soup
⅓ cup water
2 teaspoons chili powder
2 teaspoons prepared mustard
1 pound wieners, cooked
10 wiener buns, slit and toasted

Brown beef; stir to separate meat particles. Add soup, water, chili, and mustard. Heat; stir often. Place wieners in buns. Spoon soup mixture over. 10 servings.

CREAMY PEANUT BUTTER SOUP

1 can (10 fl. ounces) condensed
    tomato soup
¼ cup peanut butter (chunky or
    smooth)
1½ soup cans milk

Stir soup into peanut butter, a little at a time, until well blended; add milk. Heat; stir occasionally. 3 to 4 servings.

SUMMERTIME SPECIAL

Great after a swim

1 can (10 fl. ounces) condensed
    green pea soup
1 can (10 fl. ounces) condensed
    cream of potato soup
2 soup cans water or milk
⅛ teaspoon thyme leaves, crushed
Dash ground nutmeg

In saucepan, combine all ingredients. Heat; stir now and then. 4 to 6 servings.

WINTERTIME TREAT

Warms nose and toes

1 can (2¼ ounces) deviled ham
1 teaspoon chopped parsley
3 melba rounds
¼ cup chopped onion
1 tablespoon butter or margarine
1 can (10 fl. ounces) condensed
    green pea soup
½ soup can milk
½ soup can water

Make croûtons by combining 1 tablespoon deviled ham with parsley; spread on melba rounds. Place on cookie sheet. Broil 1 to 2 minutes. Meanwhile, cook onion in butter until tender. Blend in soup, milk, water, and remaining ham. Heat; stir often. Pour soup into bowls; top each with a croûton. 3 servings.

SLOPPY JOSÉS
Mexican Sloppy Joes!

1 pound ground beef
1 cup chopped onion
1 cup chopped celery
1 teaspoon chili powder
½ teaspoon salt
Dash pepper
1 tablespoon shortening
1 can (10 fl. ounces) condensed
 tomato soup
6 buns, split and toasted

Brown beef with onion, celery, and seasonings in shortening; stir to separate meat particles, Add soup; simmer to blend flavours. Serve on buns. 6 servings. A yummy supper served with crisp salads.

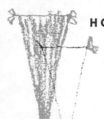

HOME-FROM-THE-GAME SUPPER

Wienerburgers*

Celery and Carrot Sticks   Pickles

Milk

Fresh Fruit   Pretzels

WIENERBURGERS

1 can (10 fl. ounces) condensed
 tomato soup
1½ pounds ground beef
1 teaspoon salt
⅛ teaspoon pepper
1½ teaspoons chili powder
6 wiener buns, split and
 toasted
6 wieners, split lengthwise
½ cup chopped onion
2 tablespoons chopped green
 pepper
2 tablespoons butter or margarine
1 tablespoon brown sugar
1 teaspoon vinegar

Combine ⅓ cup soup, beef, salt, pepper, and 1 teaspoon chili powder; mix thoroughly. Spread meat mixture evenly over buns; *cover edges completely.* Firmly press 2 wiener halves, cut side up, into the center of each bun half. Bake on broiler pan at 450°F. for 12-15 minutes. Meanwhile, in saucepan, cook onion and green pepper with remaining chili powder in butter until tender. Stir in remaining soup, sugar, and vinegar. Heat; stir now and then. Serve over sandwiches. Makes 6 open-face sandwiches.

Pizza Doggies*
Raw Vegetable Tray
Doughnuts
Cream Soda Shake

PIZZA DOGGIES

1 large clove garlic, minced
2 tablespoons olive oil
1 can (10 fl. ounces) condensed tomato soup
¼ cup water
2 tablespoons chopped parsley
¼ to ½ teaspoon leaf oregano, crushed
8 wieners, slit lengthwise
8 wiener buns, slit
6 ounces sliced Mozzarella cheese

Cook garlic in olive oil until lightly browned. Add soup, water, parsley, and oregano; cook over low heat 15 minutes. Stir often. Place wieners on buns in large shallow baking pan. Fill wieners with sauce; top with cheese. Place under broiler about 1 minute or until cheese melts. 8 servings.

PARTY DIP

1 can (10 fl. ounces) condensed cream of shrimp soup
1 package (8 ounces) cream cheese, softened
1 teaspoon lemon juice
Dash garlic powder
Dash paprika

With rotary beater or slow speed of electric mixer, gradually blend soup into remaining ingredients. Beat just until smooth. Chill. Serve as a dip with crackers or chips. Makes 2 cups dip.

BACON-TOMATO BROIL

Midnight snack for hungry dates.

4 slices toast, buttered
8 slices tomato
8 slices bacon, cooked
1 can (10 fl. ounces) condensed cream of mushroom soup
⅓ cup milk
1 teaspoon finely minced onion
½ teaspoon Worcestershire

Place toast slices on cookie sheet or in shallow baking pan; top with tomato and bacon. Stir soup until smooth. Add remaining ingredients; spoon over open-face sandwiches. Broil until bubbly. 4 servings.

111

SATURDAY NIGHT SUPPER

Chilled Cranberry Juice
Special Chicken Stack*
Fresh Fruit Cup
Rosy Rocks*
Milk and Coffee

SPECIAL CHICKEN STACK

¼ cup chopped onion
2 tablespoons butter or margarine
1 can (10 fl. ounces) condensed cream of chicken soup
⅓ cup milk
1 can (6 ounces) boned chicken, or 1 cup diced cooked chicken
2 hard-cooked eggs, sliced
4 slices buttered toast
1 package (10 ounces) frozen French style green beans, cooked

Cook onion in butter until soft but not browned; blend in soup, milk, chicken, and eggs (save several egg slices for garnish). Heat; stir often. Arrange toast on a platter; place a mound of hot beans on each slice; spoon chicken mixture over all. Garnish with egg slices. 4 servings.

BEAN 'N CORNED BEEF SPREAD

1 can (10 fl. ounces) condensed bean with bacon soup
1 cup chopped cooked corned beef
⅓ cup water
1 teaspoon prepared horseradish
1 teaspoon prepared mustard

Combine all ingredients. Spread on crunchy buttered rolls. Makes about 2 cups.

PERRITOS CON CHILE

For starving he-men

½ pound wieners, cut in ½-inch slices
½ cup chopped onion
2 tablespoons chopped green pepper
½ teaspoon chili powder
2 tablespoons butter or margarine
2 cans (19 ounces each) kidney beans, drained
1 can (10 fl. ounces) condensed tomato soup
1 teaspoon vinegar
½ teaspoon Worcestershire

Cook wieners, onion, green pepper, and chili powder in butter until wieners are browned. Add remaining ingredients. Cover; cook over low heat 12 to 15 minutes. Stir often. 6 servings. Serve with crunchy Italian bread, cheese, and a crisp salad.

SUPER-SPECIAL PICNIC

Bean 'n Bacon Burgers*
All the Trimmings
Potato Chips
Lemonade
Packaged Oatmeal Cookies

BEAN 'N BACON BURGERS

¼ cup chopped onion
2 tablespoons chopped green
   pepper
1 tablespoon butter or margarine
1 pound ground beef
1 can (10 fl. ounces) condensed
   beef with vegetables and barley
   soup
½ cup water
⅓ cup ketchup
6 hamburger buns, toasted and
   buttered

Cook onion and green pepper in butter until tender. Add beef; brown; stir to separate meat particles. Add soup, water, and ketchup; simmer about 5 minutes to blend flavours. Stir often. (Thin to desired consistency with additional water.) Serve on buns. 6 servings.

MEXICALI SUPPER

2 slices bacon
¼ cup green pepper, cut into 1-inch
   strips
1 can (10 fl. ounces) condensed
   beef with vegetables and barley
   soup
½ soup can water
1 teaspoon chili powder
⅓ cup shredded mild process cheese

Cook bacon until crisp. Remove; drain and crumble. Pour off all but 1 tablespoon drippings; add green pepper and cook until tender. Stir in soup; gradually blend in water and chili. Add cheese. Heat until cheese melts; stir often. Top with bacon. 2 servings.

SUNBATHERS' SPECIAL

Enjoy while you soak up the sun—or warm up after a cold dip

1 can (10 fl. ounces) condensed
   beef broth
½ soup can apple juice
Dash ground cinnamon or nutmeg,
   if desired

Mix ingredients and pour over ice cubes, or heat and serve hot. 2 to 3 servings.

Sandwiches—Hot and Heroic

The sandwich has come a long way since the Earl of Sandwich asked for a slice of meat between two slices of bread, to be served at the game table. Now your favourite sandwich may make a hot and hearty lunch dish or an evening snack that's truly satisfying.

Have it toasted and bubbling from the grill, or with an enticing filling spooned on. The news is in your choice of sandwich filling blended with a canned soup to make a feast-on-bread.

BROILED EGG SALAD SANDWICH

1 can (10 fl. ounces) condensed cream of mushroom soup
4 hard-cooked eggs, chopped
½ cup finely chopped celery
2 tablespoons finely chopped onion
1 tablespoon sweet pickle relish
1 teaspoon prepared mustard
Dash pepper
4 wiener buns, split and toasted

Combine soup, eggs, celery, onion, relish, mustard, and pepper. Spread mixture evenly over bun halves; *cover edges completely*. Broil about 4 inches from heat until hot, about 7 minutes. 4 open-face sandwiches.

TOMATO, CHEESE 'N BACON BROIL

8 slices bacon, cut in half
8 slices process cheese
8 slices toast
1 can (10 fl. ounces) condensed tomato soup

Partially cook bacon. Place a slice of cheese on each slice of toast; spread with soup; *cover edges completely*. Top with bacon. Broil about 4 inches from heat until cheese melts. 8 open-face sandwiches.

114

TUNABURGERS

4 slices toast or toasted buns, buttered
1 can (7 ounces) tuna, drained and flaked
4 slices onion
2 hard-cooked eggs, sliced
1 can (10 fl. ounces) condensed cream of celery soup
⅓ cup milk
2 tablespoons chopped parsley
2 teaspoons lemon juice

Place toast on cookie sheet or in shallow baking pan; spread with tuna; top with onion and egg. Combine remaining ingredients; pour over open-face sandwiches. Broil until hot. 4 servings.

WESTERN BURGER

½ cup chopped green pepper
¼ cup chopped onion
2 tablespoons butter or margarine
1 cup chopped cooked ham
1 can (10 fl. ounces) condensed cream of mushroom soup
6 eggs, slightly beaten
Dash pepper
6 buns, split and toasted

Cook green pepper and onion in butter until tender. Add ham; brown. Blend soup, eggs, and pepper; add to ham and vegetables. Cook over low heat; stir now and then until eggs are set. Serve on buns. 6 servings.

CHILIBURGER

1 pound ground beef
1 tablespoon shortening
1 can (10 fl. ounces) condensed bean with bacon soup
½ cup ketchup
½ teaspoon chili powder
6 buns, split and toasted

Brown beef in shortening; stir to separate meat particles. Add soup, ketchup, and chili powder; simmer about 5 minutes to blend flavours. Stir often. (Add a little water if desired.) Serve on buns. 6 servings.

HORSERADISH SOUPERBURGER

1 pound ground beef
1 can (10 fl. ounces) condensed cream of mushroom soup
½ cup sour cream
1 teaspoon prepared horseradish
¼ cup chopped green pepper or pimiento
6 buns, split and toasted

Brown beef in frying pan; stir often to separate meat particles. Add soup, sour cream, horseradish, and green pepper or pimiento. Simmer about 10 minutes. Serve on buns. 6 servings.

SOUPERBURGERS

1 pound ground beef
½ cup chopped onion
1 tablespoon shortening
1 can (10 fl. ounces) condensed chicken gumbo, cream of mushroom, golden mushroom, minestrone, tomato or vegetable soup
1 tablespoon prepared mustard
6 buns, split and toasted

Brown beef and onion in shortening; stir to separate meat particles. Add soup and seasoning; simmer 5 to 10 minutes to blend flavours. Stir often. Serve on buns. 6 servings.

NOTE: Decrease mustard to 1 teaspoon when using minestrone or vegetable soup.

PIZZABURGER

¼ cup chopped onion
2 tablespoons shortening
1 pound ground beef
1 can (10 fl. ounces) condensed tomato soup
½ cup shredded sharp cheese
⅛ teaspoon oregano
Dash pepper
8 buns, split and toasted

Brown onion in shortening. Add beef; cook until browned; stir often to separate meat particles. Add soup, cheese, oregano, and pepper. Simmer about 10 minutes. Serve on buns. 8 servings.

WESTERN STYLE SANDWICH

1 can (10 fl. ounces) condensed bean with bacon soup
¼ cup water
4 slices toast
4 slices tomato
4 thin slices onion
4 thin slices mild process cheese, cut into strips

Blend soup and water. Spread on toast, *covering edges completely*. Broil about 4 inches from heat for 5 minutes. Top with tomato, onion, and cheese; broil until cheese melts. 4 sandwiches.

BACON AND TOMATO SANDWICH

8 slices bacon
1 can (10 fl. ounces) condensed Cheddar cheese soup
⅓ cup milk
1 teaspoon lemon juice
Dash cayenne pepper
2 medium tomatoes, sliced
4 slices toast, buttered

Cook bacon until crisp; pour off drippings. Set aside. Stir soup into frying pan. Add milk, lemon juice, and pepper; blend until smooth. Heat slowly, stir often. Meanwhile, make open-face sandwiches by placing tomato and bacon on toast; pour hot sauce over. 4 servings.

116

WIENER AND BEAN SANDWICH

6 wiener buns, split and toasted
6 wieners, cut in half lengthwise
1 can (10 fl. ounces) condensed bean with bacon soup
⅓ cup water
¼ cup ketchup
2 tablespoons sweet pickle relish

Arrange buns on cookie sheet or in shallow baking pan; place wieners on top. Combine remaining ingredients; *spread over wieners and buns completely*. Broil until hot. 6 servings.

SHRIMP-CRAB BISQUE SANDWICHES

1 can (10 fl. ounces) condensed cream of mushroom soup
1 cup cooked crab meat, flaked
1 cup diced cooked shrimp
¼ cup finely chopped celery
¼ cup finely chopped onion
½ teaspoon lemon juice
¼ teaspoon Worcestershire
6 slices toast or rusks
3 slices (about 3 ounces) Swiss cheese, cut in half
⅓ cup milk
¼ cup finely chopped green pepper

Combine ¼ cup soup, crab, shrimp, celery, onion, lemon juice, and Worcestershire. Spread mixture evenly over toast; *cover edges completely*. Top with cheese. Broil 4 inches from heat for 5 minutes or until hot and cheese melts. Meanwhile, combine remaining soup, milk, and green pepper. Heat; stir now and then. Serve over toast. Makes 6 sandwiches.

PUMPERNICKEL-KRAUT AND WIENERS

1 can (10 fl. ounces) condensed bean with bacon soup
4 slices pumpernickel bread, lightly toasted
1½ cups sauerkraut, drained
4 wieners, slit lengthwise
¼ cup ketchup

Spread soup on bread; cover with sauerkraut. Top each sandwich with a wiener; spread with ketchup. Broil until sandwiches are hot, about 8 minutes. 4 servings.

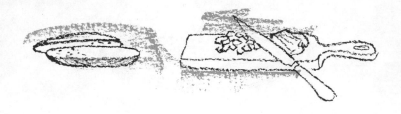

CHICKEN SPREAD-A-BURGER

1 can (10 fl. ounces) condensed cream of chicken soup
1 cup diced cooked chicken
¼ cup finely chopped celery
2 tablespoons finely chopped onion
2 tablespoons chopped pimiento
Dash pepper
4 wiener buns, split and toasted

Combine soup, chicken, celery, onion, pimiento, and pepper. Spread mixture evenly over bun halves; *cover edges completely.* Broil about 4 inches from heat until hot, about 7 minutes. 4 open-face sandwiches.

CANTONESE CHICKEN SANDWICH

½ medium onion, sliced
¼ cup sliced water chestnuts
1 tablespoon butter or margarine
1 can (10 fl. ounces) condensed cream of chicken soup
⅓ cup milk
1 tablespoon soy sauce
4 servings sliced cooked chicken or turkey
4 slices buttered toast

Cook onion and water chestnuts in butter until onion is just tender. Stir in soup, milk, and soy sauce. Heat; stir often. Arrange chicken on toast; pour sauce over. 4 servings.

CHINA BOY SANDWICH

1 can (10 fl. ounces) condensed cream of mushroom soup
1 cup diced cooked chicken
¼ cup thinly sliced celery
¼ cup sliced water chestnuts
¼ cup chopped onion
1 teaspoon soy sauce
4 wiener buns, split and toasted

Combine soup, chicken, celery, water chestnuts, onion, and soy sauce. Spread mixture evenly over bun halves; *cover edges completely.* Broil about 4 inches from heat until hot, about 7 minutes. 4 open-face sandwiches.

SAUCY QUICK SANDWICH

4 servings sliced cooked ham or chicken
4 slices toast
1 package (10 ounces) frozen asparagus spears, cooked and drained
1 can (10 fl. ounces) condensed cream of celery, chicken, mushroom, or Cheddar cheese soup
¼ to ⅓ cup milk

Place chicken on toast; top with asparagus. In saucepan, combine soup and milk. Heat; stir now and then. Pour sauce over open-face sandwiches. 4 servings.

STEAK BARBECUE

1 pound thinly sliced sirloin, cut in strips
¼ cup chopped onion
1 large clove garlic, minced
1 teaspoon barbecue seasoning
2 tablespoons butter or margarine
1 can (10 fl. ounces) condensed tomato soup
⅓ cup water
4 wiener buns, split and toasted

Cook meat, onion, garlic, and barbecue seasoning in butter until meat is browned and onion is tender. Add soup and water. Cook for 10 minutes; stir often. Serve on buns. 4 servings.

BRUNCH PANCAKE SANDWICH

4 slices bacon
1 can (10 fl. ounces) condensed cream of chicken or mushroom soup
⅓ to ½ cup milk
4 hard-cooked eggs, sliced
2 tablespoons chopped pimiento
Pancakes

Cook bacon until crisp; remove and crumble; pour off drippings. Blend soup and milk; add bacon, eggs, and pimiento. Heat; stir now and then. Serve sandwiched between pancakes. 4 servings.

Dips and Spreads

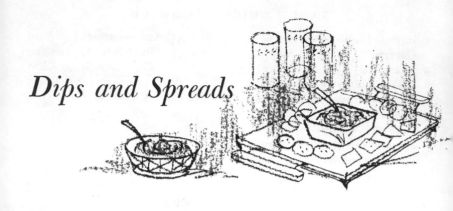

When company is coming or refrigerator-raiders descend, dips made with soup are creamy smooth, extra tasty, and extra easy. Take a can of hearty bean with bacon soup and let it form the basis for a zesty, welcoming dip . . . or choose tangy tomato soup.

Whatever your favourites, you'll enjoy teaming soup dips with assorted crackers, potato chips, pretzels, and other "dunkable munchables." For a vitamin-packed change, try using crisp carrot sticks, celery sticks, or cauliflowerets for dunking. Or let the dip double as a spread for sandwiches and hors d'oeuvres.

You can match your dip to the mood of the occasion when you choose from the variety provided by flavourful condensed soups. Just let your imagination take over.

SPANISH DIP

1 can (10 fl. ounces) condensed cream of celery soup
1 package (8 ounces) cream cheese, softened
2 tablespoons chopped green pepper
2 tablespoons chopped ripe olives
2 tablespoons finely chopped onion
¼ teaspoon Worcestershire
Generous dash hot pepper sauce

With electric mixer or rotary beater, gradually blend soup into cream cheese. Add remaining ingredients. Chill. Serve with crackers or chips. Makes about 2 cups.

DILLED DIP

1 can (10 fl. ounces) condensed
   cream of celery soup
1 package (8 ounces) cream cheese,
   softened
½ cup chopped cucumber
2 tablespoons finely chopped onion
¼ teaspoon dried dill leaves,
   crushed
⅛ teaspoon hot pepper sauce

With electric mixer or rotary beater, gradually blend soup into cream cheese. Add cucumber, onion, dill, and pepper sauce. Chill. Serve with crackers or chips. Makes about 2 cups.

NEW ENGLANDER'S SPECIAL

1 can (10 fl. ounces) condensed
   New England clam chowder soup
¼ cup chili sauce
2 tablespoons finely chopped onion
1 package (8 ounces) cream cheese,
   softened

With electric mixer or rotary beater, gradually blend soup, chili sauce, and onion into cream cheese. Chill. Serve with crackers or chips. Makes about 2½ cups.

SHRIMP BLUE CHEESE DIP

1 can (10 fl. ounces) condensed
   Cheddar cheese soup
2 tablespoons crumbled blue cheese
1 tablespoon finely chopped onion
1 teaspoon sherry
⅛ teaspoon hot pepper sauce
1 package (8 ounces) cream cheese,
   softened
Cooked shrimp

With electric mixer or rotary beater, gradually blend soup, blue cheese, onion, sherry, and hot pepper sauce into cream cheese. Chill. Serve with shrimp, crackers, or chips. Makes about 2 cups.

CREAMY BEAN DUNK

1 package (8 ounces) cream cheese,
   softened
1 can (10 fl. ounces) condensed
   bean with bacon soup
2 tablespoons grated onion
Dash hot pepper sauce
Dash garlic powder

Beat cream cheese with rotary beater or electric mixer until smooth. Gradually add remaining ingredients; blend thoroughly. Chill. Makes about 2¼ cups.

CLAM DIGGERS DUNK

1 can (10 fl. ounces) condensed
   New England clam chowder soup
1 package (8 ounces) cream cheese,
   softened
½ cup mushrooms, drained and
   chopped
1 tablespoon finely chopped onion
Dash cayenne pepper

With rotary beater or slow speed of electric mixer, gradually blend soup into cream cheese. Add remaining ingredients. Chill. Serve with crackers or chips. Makes about 2½ cups.

BACON 'N BEAN DIP

1 can (10 fl. ounces) condensed
   bean with bacon soup
¼ cup chili sauce
2 tablespoons minced green pepper,
   if desired
1 teaspoon minced onion
1 teaspoon Worcestershire

Mix all ingredients; chill. Especially tasty with bacon wafers. If smoother dip is desired, beat in electric mixer or blender. May also be used as a sandwich spread, served on toast. Makes about 1½ cups.

CREAMY CHOWDER DIP

1 can (10 fl. ounces) condensed
   New England clam chowder soup
1 medium clove garlic, minced
½ teaspoon Worcestershire
1 package (8 ounces) cream cheese,
   softened

With electric mixer or rotary beater, gradually blend soup, garlic, and Worcestershire into cream cheese; beat until just smooth. Chill. Serve with crackers or chips. Makes about 2 cups.

DEVILED DELIGHT

1 package (8 ounces) cream cheese,
   softened
1 can (10 fl. ounces) condensed
   tomato soup
2 cans (4½ ounces each) deviled
   ham
¼ cup finely chopped cucumber
2 teaspoons finely chopped green
   onion
1 small clove garlic, minced

Beat cream cheese until smooth with electric mixer or rotary beater. Add remaining ingredients; blend thoroughly. Chill. Makes about 2¼ cups. Serve as dip or spread for crackers, Melba toast, buttered bread.

Soups and the Freezer

Your freezer can be a real friend when unexpected company pops in or when your schedule's extra tight. It's so nice to know that your tasty home-made specialties are just waiting on the freezer shelf, ready to help you maintain your culinary reputation at a moment's notice. You can cut down on last-minute dinner party preparation time, too, if you make the main dish ahead of time and freeze it. It's fun to be the unruffled hostess and still come through with a delightful meal.

If frozen properly, your food will retain every bit of the fresh taste and bright colour you enjoy so much. Just remember to package your food in air and moisture-proof wrappers and containers, and to keep your freezer set at 0°F. or lower.

It's also a good idea to organize the packages in your freezer so you can find each item of food when you want it. One way is to post a list near the freezer and write down each item as you store it, checking it off when you remove it for use. This way you'll know exactly what foods you have for planning nutritious, interesting meals.

Soups contribute a great deal to households with freezers by helping with the preparation of special cooked dishes. If you're the lucky owner of a freezer, you know it's as easy to prepare a double amount of foods that freeze well—part to be eaten at once and part to be frozen. Many casseroles lend themselves especially well to this—and by using a can of soup for sauce, you can halve your cooking time. This is true also for creamed chicken and similar dishes to be frozen.

Research has shown that meats particularly freeze better when prepared with a sauce; this protects the meat from contact with air—and, therefore, aids in preventing off-flavours. Soup sauces are especially good for freezing because they retain their smooth consistency at low temperatures.

Other pointers to insure good results in freezing prepared foods are these:

1. Freeze only as much of a prepared food as you can use in one month or soon after. Generally, a fairly fast turnover is recommended by freezer specialists—rather than long storage of any food items.

2. Cool a cooked food as fast as possible and wrap it carefully so it is moistureproof.

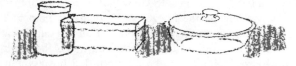

3. For packaging, you may place mixture in plastic freezer container or glass jar; leave 1-inch of head space at top because food will expand when frozen. Another method is to freeze and store the casserole mixture or similar food right in the casserole if you have one to spare. Or line a clean casserole with heavy duty aluminum foil, enough to wrap completely around the food and seal over the top. Pour in the food and seal foil with a double fold (press down tight against food). Place casserole in freezer until food is frozen solid. Then simply remove the foil-wrapped frozen food from the casserole . . . it will keep its shape and be protected in the freezer. When ready to serve the dish, remove it from foil (still frozen); put in pan to heat.

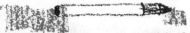

4. Freezing at 0°F. or lower is important to success with any kind of food. Put unfrozen foods in the fastest freezing area or in direct contact with freezer walls or shelves and away from already frozen foods. Place packages so air can circulate among them. Do not overload freezer with a large number of foods to be frozen at once.

5. Label each package with date, name of product, and number of servings.

6. Freeze in one package an average amount for serving your family. Large amounts take a long time to freeze—and to heat later on for serving (unless thawed completely before re-heating). Food in a large casserole may burn around the edges before it is warm in the center.

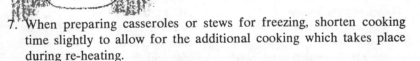

7. When preparing casseroles or stews for freezing, shorten cooking time slightly to allow for the additional cooking which takes place during re-heating.

8. To prepare a frozen main dish for serving, you may thaw it in the refrigerator—and bake as usual as soon as thawed. Or you may heat the frozen item in the oven—allowing longer heating time than specified in the original recipe (you will need to check dish during baking since no specific rule for increased baking time can be given for all dishes).

A number of dishes throughout this book have been tested for successful freezing. These include (see index):

Macaroni and Cheese—Family Style
Old Fashioned Meat Loaf (leave off topping)
Tomato Beef Stew (do not flour meat; leave out potatoes and thyme)

The following recipes also freeze well:

STROGANOFF

1 **pound round steak, cut into thin strips**
½ **cup chopped onion**
2 **tablespoons butter or margarine**
1 **can (10 fl. ounces) condensed cream of mushroom soup**
¼ **cup water**
½ **cup sour cream**
½ **teaspoon paprika**
2 **cups cooked noodles**

Brown steak and onion in butter. Stir in soup, water, sour cream, and paprika. Cover; cook over low heat 45 minutes or until meat is tender. Stir often. Serve over noodles. 4 servings.

CHILI MEATBALLS

1 **pound ground beef**
2 **tablespoons fine dry bread crumbs**
2 **tablespoons finely chopped onion**
1 **egg, slightly beaten**
1 **teaspoon chili powder**
¼ **teaspoon salt**
1 **can (10 fl. ounces) condensed tomato soup**
⅓ **cup water**
1 **small clove garlic, minced**

Mix beef, bread crumbs, onion, egg, ½ teaspoon chili powder, and salt; shape into 16 meatballs. In frying pan, brown meatballs; pour off fat. Stir in soup, water, garlic, and remaining chili powder. Cover; cook over low heat 20 minutes. Stir now and then. 4 servings.

All About Soups

Soup enhances mealtime pleasure today as it has from the beginning of time.

With condensed and ready to serve soups, you have a favourite food on hand around the clock—whether winter or summer. Try a cup or bowlful for that something new to brighten breakfast or a snacktime. Send it in a lunch box to add a note of warmth. Dress it up for a party—using a special soup mate or a gala garnish.

The following chapters cover almost every phase of modern-day soup service. Many recipes and menus are given for family meals and guest occasions.

Nourishing Soup
Through the Day

Soup can work a full day in helping you plan sound menus. Look over the following mealtime suggestions for tips on breakfast through supper:

1. CEREAL SURPRISE: Suppose, for example, Bob or Jane hits a breakfast snag. Cereal suddenly remains untouched, and the morning meal seems a bore. A bowl of Beef Soup with its nubbins of barley, bright vegetables, and meat pieces may be just the interesting contrast in taste and texture that is needed.

WARM-UP BREAKFAST
Sliced Orange
Bowl of Beef with Vegetables and
  Barley Soup
Toast and Jelly
Crisp Bacon Curls
Milk

SUNNY STARTER
Grapefruit Sections
French Toast
Mug of Tomato Soup (made
  with milk)

2. MILK BONUS: Teen-aged Sally suddenly leaves milk behind; or her father, a man of meat-and-potatoes tastes, ignores the fact that adults need a pint of milk a day, too. Most condensed soups can be heated with milk instead of water; skim milk or instant non-fat dry milk fill dieters' needs.

MILK BONUS SNACKS
Cream of Mushroom Mug
Peanut Butter Crackers
•   •   •
Cream of Tomato Cup
Cinnamon Toast

ANY DAY DINNER
Cream of Potato Soup
Ham Steak   Green Beans
Salad with Russian Dressing
Italian Bread
Apple Strudel   Sliced Cheese

3. VEGETABLE WELCOME: Billy balks at vegetables. For him, lunch or supper might start with a bowl of any one of the vegetable soups.

LUNCH BOX WINNER
Minestrone (in vacuum bottle)
Tuna Fish Sandwich
Brownies   Fruit
Milk

SUPPER SPECIAL
Chunky Vegetable Soup
Barbecued Wieners
Toasted Buns   Fresh Fruit Salad
Cookies   Milk

4. MEATLESS MENUS: Aside from the basic food values, soups help meet other special nutritional needs. On fast days or budget days, meatless meals may be planned around soups. Count on these meatless kinds: Cheddar cheese, cream soups (asparagus, celery, mushroom), green pea, tomato, old fashioned tomato rice, vegetarian vegetable, clam chowder (both styles); cream of potato, cream of shrimp, oyster stew, and chunky vegetable.

FRIDAY DINNER
Purée Mongole*
Saucy Fish Fillets*
Baked Potatoes   Buttered Broccoli
Berries in Patty Shells   Cream

OVEN SUPPER
Clam Chowder
Tuna Noodle Casserole
Baked Stuffed Tomatoes*
Spice Cake

5. PICKUPS: Secretary Sue wants a work-break at midmorning or mid-afternoon. So does Mrs. Homemaker—and almost everyone else. For many, this should be a low-calorie pause, which provides a quick pickup. Soup taken as a "work-break" has lasting advantages. Beef broth and consommé are particularly convenient and low-calorie choices, served hot or cold.

6. SOUPER SNACKS: Soup makes a "warming welcome home" to youngsters after school (try vegetable or green pea for hearty eating) . . . a great midnight snack after a movie (cosmopolitans take French onion) . . . good companion for travelers (chicken noodle and vegetable beef, the favourites) . . . and the nightcap that brings tranquil dreams (cream of chicken or chicken with rice).

PLANNING BALANCED MENUS

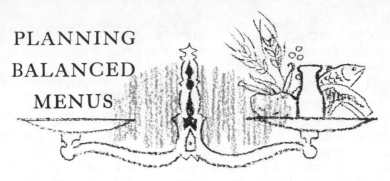

As a modern homemaker, one of your first aims in keeping your family healthy is to provide nourishing meals. You will find the many varieties of soup—from clear broths to hearty chowders—helpful in planning balanced menus. You'll be interested to see how the many soups fit into the Daily Food Guide.*

MILK GROUP:

Cream of Potato
Cream of Shrimp
New England Clam Chowder
Oyster Stew

MEAT AND FISH GROUP:

Bean with Bacon
Beef with Vegetables and Barley
Cheddar Cheese
Chunky Beef
Chunky Chicken
Chunky Turkey
Green Pea
Ox Tail

BREAD - CEREAL GROUP:

Beef Noodle
Chicken & Stars
Chicken Noodle-O's
Chunky Chicken
Golden Vegetable Noodle-O's
Noodles & Ground Beef
Tomato Noodle-O's
Turkey Noodle

FRUIT - VEGETABLE GROUPS:

Bisque of Tomato
Chicken Gumbo
Chicken Vegetable
Chunky Beef
Chunky Turkey
Chunky Vegetable
Clam Chowder Manhattan Style
French Canadian Style Pea
Golden Vegetable Noodle-O's
Minestrone
Old Fashioned Tomato Rice
Old Fashioned Vegetable
Scotch Broth
Tomato
Turkey Vegetable
Vegetable
Vegetable Beef
Vegetable, Cream of
Vegetarian Vegetable

*See Page 4

Better
Breakfasts

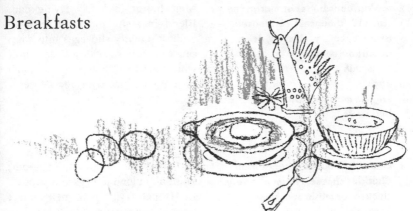

Those who know the joys of soup for breakfast—hearty, warming, invigorating—crow about their eye-openers.

Soup gives bonus flavour to more usual breakfast foods. Try eggs poached in soup. Here's breakfast news that nurtures the spirit, too!

There is also soup in a bowl or mug, heated as usual, perhaps with a generous pat of butter melting on top. Serve with crisp toast or muffin; add browned bacon or golden sausage, and fruit to round out a happy start for the day.

COLD DAY BREAKFAST
Grapefruit Half
Green Pea Soup
Coffee Cake
Cocoa

SPRING DAY BREAKFAST
Fruit in Season
Savoury Poached Eggs*
    on English Muffins
Milk or Coffee

SUMMER BREAKFAST
Half Cantaloupe
Tomato Soup (made with milk)
    with Corn Flakes on top
Buttered Toast   Ham
Milk or Coffee

AUTUMN BREAKFAST
Orange Sections
Vegetable Beef Soup
Date Nut Bread
Milk or Coffee

SAVOURY POACHED EGGS

2 tablespoons butter or margarine
1 can (10 fl. ounces) condensed
  cream of celery, chicken, or
  mushroom soup
½ cup milk
6 eggs
3 English muffins (split, toasted, and
  buttered)

Melt butter in heavy frying pan. Blend in soup and milk; heat to boiling. Gently slip eggs into soup sauce; cook over low heat until whites are firm. Place eggs on muffins. Pour sauce over eggs. 6 servings.

CAMPBELLED EGGS

1 can (10 fl. ounces) condensed
  Cheddar cheese, cream of celery,
  chicken, or mushroom soup
8 eggs, slightly beaten
Dash pepper
2 tablespoons butter or margarine

In bowl, stir soup until smooth; gradually blend in eggs and pepper. In 10-inch frying pan, melt butter; pour in egg mixture. Cook over low heat; do not stir. As mixture begins to set around edges, gently lift cooked portions with large turner so that thin, uncooked portion can flow to the bottom. Continue gently lifting cooked portions until eggs are completely set, but still moist (about 8 minutes). 4 servings.

CREAMED BRUNCH BEEF

¼ pound sliced dried beef
¼ cup chopped onion
2 tablespoons butter or margarine
1 can (10 fl. ounces) condensed
  cream of celery soup
½ cup milk
4 slices toast

Rinse dried beef in hot water; drain. Brown beef and onion in butter. Stir in soup and milk. Heat; stir often. Serve on hot toast. 4 servings.

DON FAR TONG (Egg Drop Soup)

2 cans (10 fl. ounces each)
  condensed beef broth
2 soup cans water
½ medium bay leaf
1 egg

Combine soup, water, and bay leaf. Bring to a boil. Beat egg slightly; slowly pour it in a thin stream into soup, stirring constantly. Remove bay leaf. Egg should form thin threads. Serve with toast. 4 to 6 servings.

132

Magic Menu Maker
for Lunches
and
Lunch Box Meals

Soup and sandwiches are Canadian lunchtime favourites. They offer a good way to add vegetables, meat, or milk to noon meals.

Here are some tips on packing lunches which may be helpful to you:

1. Plan a well-balanced meal with a few extras to satisfy your "luncher". Select favourite foods and food combinations—one of the best is soup and sandwiches. An occasional "surprise" would be a welcome treat. Plenty of paper napkins and colourful straws for sipping milk are other "inviting" touches for the lunch box.

2. For sandwiches, use a variety of fillings and breads. If you make up sandwiches the night before they're to be eaten, keep them refrigerated until you pack the lunch. Wrap sandwiches in moistureproof, clear lunch box wrap material or foil as soon as they are made.

3. Wrap lettuce or other moist fillings, such as sliced tomatoes, separately. Do not include salad-type meat fillings for sandwiches unless the lunch can be stored in a cool place—and will only be held for a short time.

4. Always have one hot dish. You're sure of pleasing if you include a vacuum bottle of hot soup. Any of the condensed and ready to serve soups are good to carry. And many kinds may be prepared with milk —a nutritional plus. A wide-mouth vacuum bottle is ideal for soup— easy to pour into and to eat from. Make sure the soup's hot before packing (rinse the vacuum bottle with hot water before pouring in soup). Be sure to send along a soup spoon or a long-handled spoon for eating right from the bottle.

GREAT EATING AT HOME OR AWAY

SOUPS	SANDWICHES	DESSERTS	TIPS FOR LUNCH BOX
Cream of Asparagus	Meat loaf on hard roll	Fig bars	Cut sandwich roll in half for easy eating
Bean with Bacon	Sliced ham and lettuce on rye bread	Apple	Wrap lettuce for sandwich in waxed paper
Beef with Vegetables and Barley	Swiss cheese on whole wheat bread	Peaches (fresh or canned)	Pack cole slaw in container with lid
Beef Noodle	Liverwurst and onion on white	Cherry strudel	Pack celery and carrot sticks
Chunky Beef	Sharp cheese and lettuce on white bread	Fruit tapioca	Pack a plastic fork or spoon
Cream of Celery	Salmon salad and lettuce on hard roll	Blueberry pie tart	Pack a few cherry tomatoes
Cream of Chicken	Ham and cheese— "double decker"	Grapes and oatmeal cookies	Use white and dark bread
Chicken Gumbo	Cream cheese and ham on date-nut bread	Orange	Peel and section orange; pack in sandwich bag
Chicken Noodle	Egg, bacon, and lettuce on whole wheat bread	Apple sauce cake	Add radishes or green pepper for crunch
Chicken with Rice	Salami, tomato, cheese on roll	Chocolate chip cookies	Use clear plastic wrap for sandwiches
Chunky Chicken	Peanut butter and jelly on white bread	Sliced peaches	Pack celery sticks
Clam Chowder	Egg salad on pumpernickel bread	Cherries (fresh or canned)	Pickles and olives go well with sandwiches

WITH SOUP AS A TASTY STARTER

SOUPS	SANDWICHES	DESSERTS	TIPS FOR LUNCH BOX
Chicken & Stars	Bologna, cheese, lettuce on white bread	Tomato soup cake	Add a small bag of salted nuts
French Canadian Style Pea Green Pea	Ham salad on poppyseed roll	Apricots (fresh or canned)	Keep vacuum bottle clean and "sweet"—rinse with baking soda solution
Minestrone	Sliced chicken on hard roll	Orange sections	Freeze sandwiches for lunch boxes
Cream of Mushroom	Roast beef on rye bread	Banana	Wrap crisp vegetables to munch
Ox Tail Cream of Potato	Cream cheese and dried beef on white bread	Pears (fresh or canned)	Use glass jars with tops for desserts
Scotch Broth	Luncheon loaf on rye bread	Sliced Peaches	Tuck in a small box of raisins
Tomato	Tuna salad on hard roll	Chocolate cup cake	Pack some green grapes
Old Fashioned Tomato Rice	Roast beef on white bread	Baked apple	Be sure to include a napkin or two
Turkey Noodle	Deviled ham and tomato on whole wheat bread	Lemon pie tart	Wrap slices of tomato in foil for sandwich
Turkey Vegetable Chunky Turkey	Sliced ham and cheese on rye	Butterscotch pudding	Pack cole slaw
Vegetable	Bacon, lettuce, sliced tomato on soft roll	Brownies	Wrap sandwich items separately —let "luncher" put together
Vegetable Beef	Cream cheese and olive on brown bread	Plums (fresh or canned)	Include a hard-cooked egg
Cream of Vegetable	Chicken spread and stuffed olives on roll	Fruit cocktail	Put in lettuce for sandwich
Vegetarian Vegetable	Sliced turkey, lettuce on club roll	Applesauce, Gingerbread	Put mayonnaise in small piece of foil

135

Souper Soups

Here come the heartiest, happiest, homiest soups of them all . . . the Souper Soups! Chock-full of stick-to-the-ribs goodness, these robust soups will turn an after-the-game snack into a feast, or get a light meal off to a rip-roaring start. And each has a distinct personality . . . one or more condensed soups serve as a base for a variety of substantial and savoury additions. M'm! M'm! Good!

SOUPER SOUP MENUS

Rosy Chili and Beef Soup*
Chef Salad   Corn Muffins
Blueberry Turnovers (frozen)

Chicken Pea Soup Bowl*
Fruit Salad   Rolls
Coconut Custard Pie

Seafood and Tomato Bowl*
Crackers   Cheese
Deviled Eggs   Relishes
Apple Pie Tarts (frozen)

Italian Bowl*
Antipasta
Toasted Italian Bread
Spumoni

ROSY CHILI AND BEEF SOUP

½ pound ground beef
2 tablespoons chopped onion
1 teaspoon chili powder
½ teaspoon salt
1 tablespoon butter or margarine
1 can (10 fl. ounces) condensed tomato soup
1 can (10 fl. ounces) condensed beef with vegetables and barley soup
1½ soup cans water

Combine beef, onion, chili powder, and salt; shape into 12 small meatballs. In saucepan, brown meatballs in butter. Add soups and water. Heat; stir often. 4 servings.

136

OLD FASHIONED VEGETABLE-BACON SOUP

3 slices bacon
¼ cup green pepper strips
⅛ teaspoon tarragon leaves, crushed
1 can (10 fl. ounces) condensed old fashioned vegetable soup
1 soup can water

In saucepan, cook bacon until crisp; remove and crumble. Pour off all but 1 tablespoon drippings. Cook green pepper with tarragon in drippings until tender. Add soup and water. Heat; stir now and then. Garnish with bacon. 2 to 3 servings.

SWISS POTATO SOUP

1 can (10 fl. ounces) condensed cream of potato soup
⅛ teaspoon dry mustard
1 soup can milk
½ cup shredded Swiss cheese
2 tablespoons chopped parsley

In saucepan, blend soup and mustard. Add milk, cheese, and parsley. Heat until cheese melts. Stir now and then. 2 to 3 servings.

HEARTY WIENER SOUP

2 wieners, thinly sliced
2 tablespoons chopped onion
1 tablespoon butter or margarine
1 can (10 fl. ounces) condensed old fashioned tomato rice soup
1 soup can water

Brown wieners and onion in butter. Add soup and water. Heat; stir often. 2 to 3 servings.

CREAMY SALMON SOUP

½ cup thinly sliced cucumber
2 tablespoons chopped onion
⅛ teaspoon minced dill leaves
1 tablespoon butter or margarine
1 can (10 fl. ounces) condensed cream of celery soup
1 cup water
⅓ cup sour cream
1 can (7¾ ounces) salmon, drained and flaked

Cook cucumber, onion, and dill in butter until partially tender. Add remaining ingredients. Heat. Stir often. 3 servings.

Tomato Soup, Cheese Burger.
Bean with Bacon garnished with Peas and
Hot Dog slices, Bacon Burger.

CHICKEN 'N LIMA SOUP

1 can (10 fl. ounces) condensed
   chicken vegetable soup
1 soup can milk
1 cup cooked lima beans
4 slices bacon, cooked and crumbled

Combine soup, milk, and lima beans. Heat; stir. Just before serving, add crumbled bacon. 2 to 3 servings. If desired, garnish with sliced hard-cooked egg.

TUNA POTATO CHOWDER

2 slices bacon
¼ cup chopped onion
2 tablespoons chopped green
   pepper
1 can (10 fl. ounces) condensed
   cream of potato soup
½ soup can milk
½ soup can water
1 can (7 ounces) tuna, drained and
   flaked
Dash mace

In saucepan, cook bacon until crisp; remove and crumble. Pour off all but 2 tablespoons drippings. Cook onion and green pepper in drippings until tender. Add remaining ingredients. Heat; stir now and then. Garnish with bacon. 3 servings.

CHICKEN BEEF BOWL

¼ pound sliced dried beef
½ cup chopped onion
2 tablespoons butter or margarine
1 can (10 fl. ounces) condensed
   cream of celery soup
1 can (10 fl. ounces) condensed
   cream of mushroom soup
1 soup can milk
1 soup can water
1 can (10 fl. ounces) condensed
   chicken noodle soup
1 package (12 ounces) frozen
   kernel corn, cooked and drained
Dash pepper

Shred dried beef; rinse in hot water; drain. In large saucepan, brown beef and onion in butter. Blend in cream soups, milk, and water; add remaining ingredients. Heat; stir often. 6 to 8 servings.

LOBSTER MUSHROOM SOUP

¼ cup chopped onion
2 tablespoons butter or margarine
2 cans (10 fl. ounces each) condensed cream of mushroom or celery soup
1 soup can milk
1 soup can water
1 cup flaked cooked lobster (or 5 ounce can, drained)
2 tablespoons chopped parsley
Dash pepper
Dash paprika

Cook onion in butter until tender. Blend in soup and remaining ingredients. Heat; stir often. Garnish each serving with paprika. 4 servings. NOTE: Substitute crab, salmon, shrimp, or tuna for lobster.

PEA 'N TOMATO

1 can (10 fl. ounces) condensed French Canadian style pea soup
1 can (10 fl. ounces) condensed tomato soup
1 cup milk
1 cup water

Blend soups. Gradually stir in milk and water. Heat; stir often. 4 to 6 servings.

CHICKEN PEA SOUP BOWL

1 small onion, sliced
⅛ teaspoon nutmeg
2 tablespoons butter or margarine
1 can (10 fl. ounces) condensed cream of chicken soup
1 can (10 fl. ounces) condensed green pea soup
1 can (6 ounces) boned chicken or turkey, or 1 cup diced cooked chicken or turkey
1 cup cooked sliced carrots
1 cup chopped spinach
1 ½ soup cans water

Cook onion and nutmeg in butter until onion is tender. Add remaining ingredients. Cover; simmer 5 minutes; stir often. 4 servings.

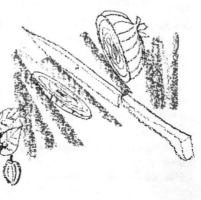

SOUP PLUS

A pattern recipe to use as you like with foods you have on hand.

½ cup cooked meat, cut in strips
1 tablespoon butter or margarine
1 can any Campbell's Soup
1 soup can milk or water
½ cup cooked vegetables

Cook meat in butter until lightly browned. Add remaining ingredients. Heat; stir often. 2 to 3 servings.

BEAN AND SAUSAGE SOUP

1 or 2 small sausage links (about 2 ounces)
1 can (10 fl. ounces) condensed bean with bacon soup
1 soup can water
Cubes of red apple

Cut sausage into ½-inch slices; brown in saucepan; pour off drippings. Blend in soup and water. Heat; stir often. Top each serving with apple cubes. 2 to 3 servings.

ITALIAN BOWL

½ pound link sausage, cut into small pieces
2 cans (10 fl. ounces each) condensed minestrone soup
1 can (10 fl. ounces) condensed tomato soup
3 soup cans water
Croûtons

In saucepan, cook sausage until done. Pour off fat. Add soups and water. Heat; stir now and then. Top with croûtons. 6 servings.

SEAFOOD AND TOMATO BOWL

¼ cup chopped onion
1 small clove garlic, minced
1 tablespoon butter or margarine
1 can (10 fl. ounces) condensed clam chowder Manhattan style
1 can (10 fl. ounces) condensed old fashioned tomato rice soup
1½ soup cans water
1 can (7 ounces) tuna, drained and flaked
2 tablespoons chopped parsley

Cook onion and garlic in butter until onion is tender. Add remaining ingredients. Heat; stir often. 4 servings.

SAUSAGE MINESTRONE

2 or 3 sausage links (about 3
   ounces), cut into thick slices
1 can (10 fl. ounces) condensed
   minestrone soup
1 soup can water

Brown sausage slices lightly; pour
off drippings. Add soup and water.
Heat; stir often. 2 to 3 servings.

CHICKEN CORN CHOWDER

1 can (10 fl. ounces) condensed
   cream of chicken soup
2 soup cans milk
1 can (10 fl. ounces) condensed
   chicken noodle soup
1 can (14 ounces) cream-style corn
1 can (6 ounces) boned chicken, or
   1 cup diced cooked chicken

Blend cream of chicken soup and
milk. Add remaining ingredients.
Heat; stir. 4 servings.

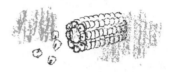

BACON AND VEGETABLE POTAGE

½ cup back bacon, cut in strips
¼ cup chopped onion
⅛ teaspoon ground sage
1 tablespoon butter or margarine
1 can (10 fl. ounces) condensed
   cream of chicken soup
1 can (10 fl. ounces) condensed
   vegetarian vegetable soup
1 soup can water
½ soup can milk
½ cup cooked chopped spinach

Cook bacon, onion, and sage in butter until bacon is browned and
onion is tender. Blend in remaining
ingredients. Heat; stir often. 4 to 6
servings.

WIENER AND BEAN SOUP

2 to 4 wieners, thinly sliced
1 tablespoon butter or margarine
1 can (10 fl. ounces) condensed
   bean with bacon soup
1 can (10 fl. ounces) condensed
   green pea soup
1 soup can milk
1 soup can water

Lightly brown wiener slices in butter. Blend in remaining ingredients.
Heat; stir. 4 to 6 servings. If desired, 1 cup diced cooked carrots may
also be added.

Youngsters Like Soup

From the toddling stage on, kids love soup. Among one-year-olds, 4 out of 10 eat soup; 7 out of 10 two-year-olds eat soup!

From split style to swirly, there's a soup for all kidfolk. Soup fits into menus for youngsters year 'round . . . for lunchboxes, snacks, camp-outs, and cook-outs.

"Growing-up" soups may be given to your baby when he's ready for soft chewing foods. Some recommended by doctors include: cream of asparagus, cream of celery, beef with vegetables and barley, beef noodle, chicken noodle, chicken with rice, green pea, Scotch broth, tomato, vegetable, vegetable beef, vegetarian vegetable, chicken vegetable, and turkey noodle.

Split style is an easy way for the very young one to eat soup. Make up soup with milk and heat thoroughly. Pour the nutritious broth into a cup for drinking; spoon the colourful solids into a plate for eating.

Birthday soup: Gay bowls of cream soup take on a party air when topped with a glowing birthday candle (set on a floating round of toast or a cracker). First top the cracker with a small ball of cream cheese or peanut butter. Poke the end of the candle into it and carefully slip the cracker onto the top of the soup. Then light up the candle.

Swirly soups: Exciting to do and nourishing too. Let the youngsters swirl or write on the soup surface this way. Prepare soup as usual and pour into bowls. Slowly pour light cream, milk, reconstituted dry milk, or evaporated milk from a pitcher, back and forth across the soup. Stir with a soup spoon to make initials, animals, faces, or pretty marbled effects.

Snippets: Good eating with soup are snippets of cheese. These are simply animals, numbers, stars, or other shapes that youngsters cut with cookie cutters from slices of process cheese. These float atop soup.

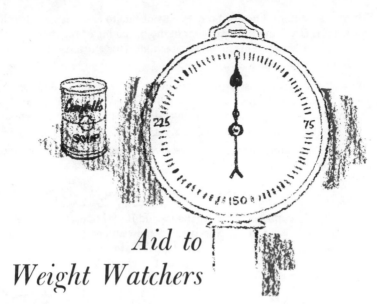

Aid to Weight Watchers

Calorie-conscious folks (wanting to lose or gain weight) can look over the following groupings of soup to see what the calories are.

Calories listed are per 1 cup portion of prepared soup (based on the first directions listed on the label).

25 to 60 CALORIES: Beef broth, chicken gumbo, chicken with rice, chicken & stars, consommé, onion.

60 to 80 CALORIES: Cream of asparagus, beef noodle, cream of celery, chicken noodle, chicken noodle-O's, chicken vegetable, clam chowder Manhattan style, golden mushroom, golden vegetable noodle-O's, old fashioned vegetable, tomato, turkey noodle, turkey vegetable, vegetable, vegetable beef, vegetarian vegetable.

80 to 100 CALORIES: Beef with vegetables and barley, cream of chicken, minestrone, noodles & ground beef, old fashioned tomato rice, Scotch broth.

100 to 125 CALORIES: Bisque of tomato, cream of potato, tomato noodle-O's, chunky turkey, chunky vegetable.

125 to 150 CALORIES: Cheddar cheese, cream of mushroom, green pea, oyster stew.

150 to 185 CALORIES: Bean with bacon, New England clam chowder, chunky beef, chunky chicken.

For the slender: Those who need lots of fuel to keep fit will also find soup a help. It is a delightful appetizer at the beginning of the meal. Too, it may be enjoyed between meals and at bedtime (for extra calories, a little butter or cream may be added to soup).

Low-calorie tips: Many of the soups team up with sandwiches and salads or desserts and non-fat (skim) milk to make well-balanced, low-calorie meals. Two soups . . . beef broth and consommé . . . are low enough in calories to be listed among the "free foods" for dieters to enjoy anytime.

Here are two simple menus for low-calorie meals, each equal to about 400 calories.

SOUP AND SANDWICH

¾ cup Beef with Vegetables and Barley Soup
Open-Face Sliced Egg Sandwich on
Rye Bread, Green Pepper Garnish
1 Glass Skim Milk or Buttermilk
1 Portion Fresh Fruit

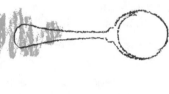

SOUP AND SALAD

¾ cup Cream of Celery Soup,
Prepared with Milk, 2 Saltines
Cold plate—2 ounces Sliced Lean Meat,
Chicken, or Turkey
Sliced Tomato and Dill Pickle Garnish
½ cup Orange and Grapefruit Compote

Low-calorie soups can be extra-flavourful, as in these recipes:

BEEF BROTH CHABLIS

1 **can (10 fl. ounces) condensed beef broth**
1 **soup can water**
2 **tablespoons Chablis or other dry white wine**

Combine all ingredients. Place in refrigerator for at least 4 hours. Serve in chilled cups or glasses. 3 servings. Calories per serving: about 35.

ENERGY BOOSTER

1 can (10 fl. ounces) condensed
    tomato soup
1 soup can water
1 bay leaf
¼ teaspoon celery salt

Combine all ingredients. Heat; simmer a few minutes to blend flavours. Remove bay leaf. 3 mugs. Calories per serving: about 75.

CRESS BROTH

1 can (10 fl. ounces) condensed
    beef broth
½ to 1 soup can water
2 tablespoons minced watercress
Lemon wedges

Combine beef broth, water, and watercress. Place in refrigerator for at least 4 hours. Serve in chilled mugs or bowls; garnish with lemon wedges. 2 to 3 servings. Calories per serving: about 35.
VARIATION: Try this with tomato soup, too.

SPINACH TOMATO SOUP

1 cup chopped fresh spinach
1 tablespoon butter or margarine
1 can (10 fl. ounces) condensed
    tomato soup
1 soup can milk or water
¼ teaspoon ground nutmeg

Cook spinach in butter 5 minutes. Blend in soup, liquid, and nutmeg. Heat; stir now and then. 3 servings. Calories per serving: about 112.

CHICKEN VEGETABLE "V-8"

1 can (10 fl. ounces) condensed
    chicken vegetable soup
½ soup can "V-8" juice
½ soup can water

Combine soup, "V-8" juice, and water. Heat; stir now and then. 3 servings. Calories per serving: about 74.

BROTH PICK-UP

1 can (10 fl. ounces) condensed
    beef broth
1 can (10 fl. ounces) condensed
    tomato soup
1 soup can water
½ teaspoon lemon juice
⅛ teaspoon sweet basil

Combine all ingredients. Heat; simmer a few minutes. Stir now and then. 3 to 4 servings. Calories per serving for 3: about 93; for 4: about 69.

Appetizer Soups

"Soup puts the heart at ease, calms down the violence of hunger, eliminates the tensions of the day, and awakens and refines the appetite."—Escoffier.

Soup, hot or chilled, sets the mood for the meal to come. Soup can breathe of spring, or bring warmth to a cold winter's evening. Cool jellied consommé revives summer appetites, and robust soups add substance to an autumn meal. Bright soup can give the colour contrast needed for a pale table setting. Clear broth is the gourmet's choice to set off elegant dinners. A tureen of soup makes a popular addition to a buffet, and the most welcome centerpiece of all, when the family gathers at the table. Happy is the family that can answer yes to

> "Do daily soups
> Your dinners introduce?"— John Gay

TOMATO MINESTRONE

1 can (10 fl. ounces) condensed
  minestrone soup
½ soup can water
½ soup can tomato juice

Combine all ingredients. Heat. 2 to 3 servings.

NUTMEG MUG

1 can (10 fl. ounces) condensed
   green pea soup
1 soup can water or milk
⅛ to ¼ teaspoon ground nutmeg
Orange slices, cut in quarters

Combine soup, water or milk, and nutmeg. Heat; stir now and then. Serve in mugs or cups; garnish with orange slices. 2 to 3 servings.

WHITE PUFF PEA SOUP

1 can (10 fl. ounces) condensed
   green pea soup
1 soup can water
Dash ground cloves
1 teaspoon grated orange rind
⅓ cup heavy cream, whipped

In saucepan, combine soup, water, and cloves. Heat; stir now and then. Fold orange rind into whipped cream. Top each serving with whipped cream. 2 to 3 servings.

SOUP ITALIANO

1 can (10 fl. ounces) condensed
   green pea soup
1 can (10 fl. ounces) condensed
   tomato soup
1½ soup cans water
2 tablespoons Chianti or other dry
   red wine (optional)
⅛ teaspoon Italian herb blend

Blend soups; add remaining ingredients. Cook over low heat 10 minutes; stir often. 4 servings. Serve with crackers topped with Mozzarella cheese, sprinkled with oregano and browned under the broiler.

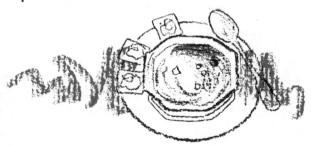

CREOLE SOUP

2 slices bacon
2 tablespoons chopped onion
1 can (10 fl. ounces) condensed
   old fashioned tomato rice soup
1 soup can water
½ cup cooked cut green beans

Cook bacon until crisp; remove and crumble. Pour off excess drippings. Add onion; cook until tender. Add soup, water, green beans, and most of bacon. Heat; stir. Sprinkle with bacon. 2 to 3 servings.

CHILLED MINTED PEA SOUP

1 can (10 fl. ounces) condensed
  green pea soup
1 soup can milk
¼ cup light cream
½ teaspoon dried mint flakes,
  crushed

Blend all ingredients. Chill at least
4 hours. 3 to 4 servings.

ROSY TURKEY NOODLE SOUP

1 can (10 fl. ounces) condensed
  turkey noodle soup
½ soup can water
½ soup can "V-8" juice

Combine all ingredients. Heat. 2 to
3 servings.

CHEESE-TOMATO

1 can (10 fl. ounces) condensed
  Cheddar cheese soup
1 can (10 fl. ounces) condensed
  tomato soup
2 soup cans water

Stir cheese soup until smooth; gradually blend in tomato soup and
water. Heat; stir often. 4 to 6 servings.

SUPPER PARTY STARTER

1 can (10 fl. ounces) condensed
  beef broth
1 soup can water
2 tablespoons wine (sauterne,
  sherry, rosé, or Burgundy)
Orange or lemon slices, clove
  studded

Combine beef broth and water; add
wine. Heat a few minutes to blend
flavours. Float clove-studded
orange or lemon slices in broth for
a colourful touch of that special
something guests appreciate. 2 to 3
servings.

CONSOMMÉ JULIENNE

1 cup vegetables cut in thin strips
  (carrot, onion, green pepper,
  leek, parsnip)
1 tablespoon butter or margarine
2 cans (10 fl. ounces each)
  condensed consommé
2 soup cans water

Choose vegetables for variety in
colour and flavour. Cook in butter
with cover on, over very low heat,
until tender but still firm. Add consommé and water. Heat; stir. 4 to
6 servings.

SAVOURY CHILLED MUSHROOM BOWL

1 can (10 fl. ounces) condensed
  cream of mushroom soup
1 soup can milk
1 teaspoon minced chives or
  chopped fresh dill
Sour cream, if desired

Blend soup, milk, and seasoning. Chill at least 4 hours. Serve in chilled bowls. Garnish with dollop of sour cream. 2 to 3 servings.

POTATO BROCCOLI BOWL

1 can (10 fl. ounces) condensed
  cream of potato soup
1 soup can milk
Dash ground nutmeg
Dash pepper
½ cup chopped cooked broccoli

In saucepan, combine soup, milk, and seasonings. Heat; stir now and then. Do not boil. Add broccoli; heat. 3 to 4 servings. Chill before serving.

CREAMY POTATO POTAGE

½ cup finely chopped cucumber
2 tablespoons chopped green onion
2 tablespoons butter or margarine
1 can (10 fl. ounces) condensed
  cream of potato soup
½ soup can milk
½ soup can water
⅓ cup sour cream
⅛ teaspoon paprika

In saucepan, cook cucumber and green onion in butter until tender. Add remaining ingredients. Heat; stir now and then. 2 to 3 servings. To serve as cold soup, prepare as above. Chill 4 hours. Thin to desired consistency with milk.

QUICK MARITIME CHOWDER

2 tablespoons chopped onion
⅛ teaspoon thyme leaves, crushed
2 tablespoons butter or margarine
1 can (10 fl. ounces) condensed
  New England clam chowder soup
1 soup can milk
½ cup cooked peas

In saucepan, cook onion with thyme in butter until tender. Add soup, milk, and peas. Heat; stir now and then. 2 to 3 servings.

PARSLEY-SHRIMP SOUP

1 can (10 fl. ounces) condensed
  cream of celery soup
1 soup can water
1 cup diced cooked shrimp
2 tablespoons chopped parsley
1 small clove garlic, minced

In saucepan, combine all ingredients. Heat; stir now and then. 3 servings.

SPRIG O' SPRING SOUP

1 can (10 fl. ounces) condensed
   cream of asparagus soup
1 soup can milk
¼ bunch watercress (about ¼ cup)
⅛ teaspoon basil
Dash pepper

Blend all ingredients 2 minutes in electric blender, or chop watercress very fine and combine with other ingredients in saucepan. Heat; stir now and then. Garnish with sprigs of watercress. 2 to 3 servings.

HOT BUTTERED SOUP

1 can (10 fl. ounces) condensed
   tomato soup
1 soup can water or milk
Butter

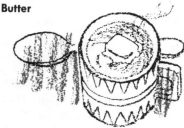

Combine soup and water. Heat; stir now and then. Pour into cups or mugs; garnish each with a pat of butter. 2 to 3 servings. Try a melt-in-your-soup butter pat atop cream of asparagus, celery, chicken, mushroom, and green pea soups, too, for extra cold or extra hungry soupsters.

BEEF BROTH WITH HORSERADISH

1 can (10 fl. ounces) condensed
   beef broth
1 cup water
½ teaspoon prepared horseradish
⅛ teaspoon dried dill leaves
Sour cream
Cucumber strips

Combine soup, water, horseradish, and dill. Simmer a few minutes. Pour into cups or mugs and top each serving with dab of sour cream. Use cucumber strips as crisp stirrers. 2 to 3 servings.

BEEF BROTH PLUS

1 can (10 fl. ounces) condensed
   beef broth
1 can (10 fl. ounces) condensed
   green pea soup
1 can (10 fl. ounces) condensed
   tomato soup
1 soup can milk
1 tablespoon sherry (optional)
Crumbled bacon, if desired

Blend beef broth and green pea soups. Add tomato soup, milk, and sherry. Heat. Add a crunchy garnish of crumbled bacon. 4 to 6 servings.

TOMATO-VEGETABLE

1 can (10 fl. ounces) condensed
tomato soup
1 can (10 fl. ounces) condensed
vegetarian vegetable soup
1 ½ soup cans water

Combine soups and water. Heat;
stir often. 4 servings.

VEGETABLE BROTH

1 can (10 fl. ounces) condensed
beef broth
1 can (10 ounces) "V-8" juice
1 teaspoon lemon juice
⅛ teaspoon sweet basil, crushed

Combine beef broth, "V-8", lemon
juice, and basil. Simmer 1 or 2
minutes. 2 to 3 servings.

HAM 'N CHICKEN CHOWDER

½ cup cooked ham, cut in strips
1 tablespoon butter or margarine
1 can (10 fl. ounces) condensed
cream of chicken soup
1 soup can water
½ cup cooked mixed vegetables

Cook ham in butter until lightly
browned. Add remaining ingredients. Heat; stir often. 2 to 3 servings.

CHILLED TOMATO BOWL

1 can (10 fl. ounces) condensed
consommé
1 can (10 fl. ounces) condensed
tomato soup
½ soup can water
½ cup chopped cucumber
½ teaspoon dried chives, crushed
Dash "Tabasco" sauce
Sour cream, if desired

Blend soups and water; add cucumber, chives, and "Tabasco" sauce.
Chill 4 hours. Serve with sour
cream afloat. 4 generous servings.

BEEF NOODLE-VEGETABLE

1 can (10 fl. ounces) condensed
beef noodle soup
1 can (10 fl. ounces) condensed
vegetable soup
1 ½ soup cans water

Combine soups and water. Heat;
stir often. 4 servings.

CREAMY CHEESE BOWL

1 can (10 fl. ounces) condensed
   cream of chicken soup
1 soup can water
1 cup shredded mild process cheese
2 tablespoons sauterne or other dry
   white wine (optional)
⅛ teaspoon garlic powder

Combine all ingredients. Heat; stir
often until cheese is melted. 2 to 3
servings.

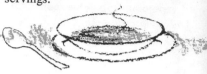

CHICKEN SOUP AMANDINE

1 can (10 fl. ounces) condensed
   cream of chicken soup
1 soup can milk
¼ teaspoon grated onion
2 tablespoons chopped toasted
   almonds

Combine soup, milk, and onion.
Heat. Garnish with almonds. 2 to 3
servings.

CURRIED CHICKEN SOUP

2 tablespoons chopped onion
1 tablespoon diced celery
1 to 2 teaspoons curry powder
1 tablespoon butter or margarine
1 can (10 fl. ounces) condensed
   cream of chicken soup
½ soup can milk
½ soup can water
Toasted almonds or coconut

In saucepan, cook onion and celery
with curry powder in butter until
tender. Blend in soup, milk, and
water. Heat; stir now and then.
Garnish with almonds or coconut.
2 to 3 servings.

GUMBO BOWL

1 can (10 fl. ounces) condensed
   chicken gumbo soup
½ soup can tomato juice
½ soup can water

Combine all ingredients. Heat; stir.
2 to 3 servings.

HERB CONSOMMÉ

1 can (10 fl. ounces) condensed
   consommé
1 soup can water
Dash dill seed, tarragon, or basil

Combine all ingredients. Heat;
simmer a few minutes. Garnish, if
desired, with toast squares. 2 to 3
servings.

CURRIED COCONUT SHRIMP SOUP

2 teaspoons butter or margarine
¼ teaspoon curry powder
¼ cup flaked coconut
1 can (10 fl. ounces) condensed cream of chicken soup
1 soup can milk
1 cup diced cooked shrimp

In small saucepan, melt butter; stir in curry powder; add coconut. Cook, stirring until lightly toasted. Meanwhile, in another saucepan, combine remaining ingredients. Heat; stir now and then. Garnish with curried coconut. 2 to 3 servings.

SEASIDE SIPPER

2 cans (10 fl. ounces each) condensed tomato soup
1 cup clam juice
1 soup can water
¼ teaspoon leaf thyme, crushed

Combine all ingredients. Heat; stir. Serve in cups or mugs. 4 to 6 servings.

TANGY TOMATO SOUP

1 can (10 fl. ounces) condensed tomato soup
1 soup can water
½ teaspoon prepared horseradish
¼ teaspoon Worcestershire
Dash dry mustard

Combine all ingredients. Simmer 5 minutes; stir often. 2 to 3 servings.

BUTTERMILK BREW

1 can (10 fl. ounces) condensed tomato soup
1 cup water
⅓ cup buttermilk
¼ cup chopped cucumber
⅛ teaspoon dill seed

Combine all ingredients. Heat; stir now and then. 2 to 3 servings.

EAST INDIA TOMATO SOUP

2 tablespoons thinly sliced green onion
1 tablespoon butter or margarine
1 can (10 fl. ounces) condensed tomato soup
1 soup can water
¼ teaspoon curry powder

Cook green onion in butter until lightly browned. Add soup, water, and curry powder. Heat; stir. Serve hot or chill at least 4 hours and serve. 2 to 3 servings.

HEARTY BEEF WARM-UP

½ cup sliced mushrooms
1 small green pepper, sliced
1 tablespoon butter or margarine
1 can (10 fl. ounces) condensed
  beef noodle soup
1 can (10 fl. ounces) condensed
  beef with vegetables and barley
  soup
1 ½ soup cans water

Cook mushrooms and green pepper in butter until tender. Add soups and water. Heat. 4 servings.

CHRISTMAS NOODLE CUP

1 can (10 fl. ounces) condensed
  beef noodle soup
1 soup can water
1 teaspoon finely chopped parsley
1 teaspoon chopped pimiento

Combine all ingredients. Heat; stir often. Garnish with wreath of chopped parsley or red bell cut from pimiento. 2 to 3 servings.

PEA SOUP PARISIAN

1 can (10 fl. ounces) condensed
  French Canadian style pea soup
1 soup can water
½ teaspoon minced instant onion
½ teaspoon lemon juice
¼ cup sour cream
1 ½ teaspoons chopped parsley
1 ½ teaspoons chopped radish

Combine soup, water, onion, and lemon juice. Heat; stir now and then. Meanwhile, combine sour cream, parsley, and radish; float on soup as a bright, contrasting garnish. 2 to 3 servings.

CELERY-CLOVE COMBO

1 can (10 fl. ounces) condensed
  cream of celery soup
1 can (10 fl. ounces) condensed
  tomato soup
1 cup water
1 cup milk
Dash ground cloves
Chopped toasted almonds, if desired

Blend soups, water, milk, and cloves. Heat; stir now and then until "serving hot", then sprinkle each serving with chopped almonds. 4 servings.

"V-8" VEGETABLE POTAGE

1 can (10 fl. ounces) condensed
   vegetable soup
½ soup can "V-8" juice
½ soup can water

Combine all ingredients. Heat. Garnish with popcorn, if desired. 2 to 3 servings.

CREME CELERY-TOMATO

1 can (10 fl. ounces) condensed
   cream of celery soup
1 soup can water
½ cup chopped tomato
2 tablespoons chopped green onion
2 tablespoons chopped green
   pepper
¼ cup sour cream

Combine all ingredients; chill. Serve in chilled bowls. 3 to 4 servings.

COUNTRY FAIR SOUP

¼ cup diced cooked ham
1 tablespoon butter or margarine
Dash ground marjoram, if desired
1 can (10 fl. ounces) condensed
   turkey vegetable soup
1 soup can water

Brown ham in butter with marjoram. Add soup and water. Heat. 2 to 3 servings.

SOUP MATES...MIX-MATCH SOUPS

One soup	*+Second soup*	*+Liquid*	*=Soup Mate*
Cream of Asparagus	Cream of Chicken	1½ cans milk or water	Heat, stir. Garnish with shreds of orange peel.
Cream of Asparagus	Scotch Broth	1½ cans water	Heat, stir. New lunch flavour.
Bean with Bacon	Minestrone	1½ cans water	Heat, stir. Ladle from bean pot.
Beef with Vegetables and Barley	Ox-Tail	2 cans water	Heat, stir. Dot with popcorn.
Beef with Vegetables and Barley	Tomato	2 cans water	Heat, stir. Add 1 teaspoon sherry, if desired. Top with chopped parsley or chives.
Beef with Vegetables and Barley	Old Fashioned Tomato Rice	1½ cans water	Heat, stir. Winter picnic warm-up.
Beef Broth	Beef Noodle	1½ cans water	Heat, stir. Topping of herb-seasoned stuffing.
Beef Broth	Tomato	1½ cans water	Heat, stir. Float toast squares on top.
Beef Noodle	Minestrone	2 cans water	Heat, stir. Pack in lunchbox in vacuum.
Beef Noodle	Tomato	1½ cans water	Heat, stir. Ladle from bright casserole.
Beef Noodle	Vegetable Beef	1½ cans water	Heat, stir. Sprinkle with grated cheese.
Cheddar Cheese	Tomato	1½ to 2 cans water	Heat, stir. Elegant in chowder mugs.
Chicken & Stars	Chicken Noodle	2 cans water	Heat. This makes a soup fit for any party theme.
Chicken Noodle	Vegetarian Vegetable	1½ cans water	Heat, stir. Accompaniment to cold sliced beef.
Chicken with Rice	Tomato	1½ cans water	Heat, stir. China soup cups on silver tray.
Chicken Vegetable	Golden Vegetable Noodle-O's	1½ to 2 cans water	Heat, stir. Cheese cubes afloat.
Cream of Celery	Chicken Vegetable	1 can water and 1 can milk	Heat, stir. Stirrers: cucumber spears.
Cream of Chicken	Chicken Noodle-O's	2 cans water or milk	Heat, stir. Add dash of curry or coconut, if desired.
Cream of Chicken	Chicken with Rice	1½ to 2 cans water or milk	Heat, stir. Break in breakfast routine; top with crisp cereal.

SOUP MATES...MIX-MATCH SOUPS

One soup	+Second soup	+Liquid	=Soup Mate
Cream of Mushroom	Cream of Asparagus	2 cans milk, or 1 can milk and 1 can water	Stir mushroom soup to smooth. Blend in asparagus soup and liquid. Heat; stir. Top with watercress.
Cream of Mushroom	Chicken with Rice	1½ cans milk or water	Stir mushroom soup to smooth. Blend in other soup and liquid. Heat, stir. Form family "soup line."
Cream of Mushroom	Consommé	1½ cans water	Stir mushroom soup to smooth. Blend in other soup and liquid. Heat, stir. Top with toasted almonds.
Cream of Vegetable	Vegetable	1½ to 2 cans water	Heat, stir. Perfect party appetizer.
Tomato Noodle-O's	Vegetable	2 cans water	Heat, stir. Serve with garnish of sieved egg yolk.
Consommé	Scotch Broth	1½ cans water	Heat, stir. Cheese crackers to munch.
Consommé	Bisque of Tomato	1½ cans water	Mix and heat. Garnish with sour cream.
French Canadian Style Pea	Consommé	1½ cans water	Heat, stir. Garnish with lemon slices.
Green Pea	Scotch Broth	1½ cans water	Heat, stir. Serve with party rye slices.
Noodles & Ground Beef	Old Fashioned Vegetable	2 cans water	Heat this hearty combination to enjoy with egg salad sandwich.
Onion	Ox Tail	1½ cans water	Good with French bread.
Onion	Vegetable Beef	2 cans water	Heat, stir. Pass crackers.
Tomato	Vegetable Beef	2 cans water	Heat, stir. Savour at Saturday lunch.
Turkey Noodle	Vegetable	1½ cans water	Heat, stir. Keep warm in chafing dish or electric kettle.

Great Soups

Almost every country has a great soup that uses the best of its lands and seas.

In French port towns, bouillabaisse holds the best of the seafood catch; in French farm country, the green pea and onion contribute to distinctive potages. In Scotland, barley goes into the broth; in India, curry flavours soup.

In Maryland, U.S.A., the crab makes a great bisque; in New England, clam is the chowder choice. Everywhere in North America, the ruddy farm tomato becomes the nation's favourite soup.

How did great soups win their claim to fame? There is much food history on this fascinating subject. For example, back in the twelfth century, soup-making became such an art that sometimes five or six kinds were served at a single meal!

A famous restaurant of long ago served only soup. The year was 1765, the place Paris. An enterprising tradesman, Monsieur Boulanger, offered what he called "restaurantes" or pickups—bowls of soup which could be bought at any hour. His soups were so popular, other people copied the custom, and eventually other prepared dishes were offered as well. With canned soups handy, you can offer "restaurantes" at any hour, too.

Let great soups from around the world be part of your family meals. Have fun cooking these modern versions.

CLAM CHOWDER

Clam chowder, named for the French *chaudier* in which it was cooked in Brittany, is canned now in creamy New England style as well as rosy Manhattan variety with tomatoes and other vegetables . . . and never the partisans of each shall meet. Both appetites can be readily satisfied. Prepared chowders are quick to heat and serve, making, as an old recipe puts it, "a dish fit for the best of the nation".

MULLIGATAWNY SOUP

Mulligatawny means "Pepper water" in India, a curry-flavoured soup.

2 cans (10 fl. ounces each) condensed cream of chicken soup

1 can (10 fl. ounces) condensed chicken with rice soup

1 ½ soup cans water

½ to 1 teaspoon curry powder

Blend soups, water, and curry powder. Heat; stir occasionally. 6 servings.

QUICK MOCK BOUILLABAISSE

Streamlined version of the fish stew native to Marseilles.

1 small onion, sliced

1 small clove garlic, minced

½ small bay leaf

¼ teaspoon thyme, crushed

2 tablespoons olive oil

1 can (10 fl. ounces) condensed tomato soup

1 soup can water

2 cups cooked seafood (crab, fish, lobster, shrimp)

1 teaspoon lemon juice

Dash "Tabasco" sauce

4 slices French bread, toasted

Cook onion, garlic, bay leaf, and thyme in olive oil until onion is tender. Add soup, water, seafood (any combination you like), lemon juice, and "Tabasco" sauce. Bring to boil. Cover; simmer 5 minutes. To serve: ladle soup over toast in bowls. 3 to 4 servings.

POT-O-GOLD SOUP

1 can (10 fl. ounces) condensed consommé

3 cups sliced raw carrots (about 1 pound)

¼ cup chopped celery

2 tablespoons chopped onion

1 soup can light cream

½ soup can milk

¼ teaspoon nutmeg

In saucepan, combine consommé, carrots, celery, and onion. Cover; cook 20 minutes or until carrots are very tender. Blend in electric blender until smooth. In saucepan, combine all ingredients. Heat; stir now and then. 3 servings.

CIOPPINO

Glorified fish soup, a specialty at British Columbian Fisherman's Wharfs.

½ cup chopped green pepper
½ cup chopped onion
2 tablespoons chopped parsley
2 cloves garlic, minced
¼ cup olive oil
2 cans (10 fl. ounces each)
  condensed tomato soup
1 soup can water
¼ teaspoon basil, crushed
1 bay leaf
¼ teaspoon grated lemon rind
⅛ teaspoon salt
Dash pepper
¼ cup dry white wine (optional)
1 pound haddock fillets, cut in
  2-inch pieces
1 pound fresh shrimp, shelled
½ pound cooked crab meat

Cook green pepper, onion, parsley, and garlic in olive oil until vegetables are tender. Stir in soup, water, basil, bay leaf, lemon rind, salt, and pepper. Cook over low heat about 10 minutes to blend flavours. Add remaining ingredients. Cook 10 minutes more. Stir gently now and then. 6 to 8 servings.

NOVA SCOTIA BISQUE

A Peninsula blend of seafood flavours you can make quickly.

2 cans (10 fl. ounces each)
  condensed oyster stew
2 soup cans milk
2 cups diced cooked potatoes
2 tablespoons chopped parsley

In saucepan, combine all ingredients. Heat; stir now and then. 4 to 6 servings.

PRAIRIE CHOWDER

A hearty, rugged inland blend of what's handy for the big soup pot.

1 can (10 fl. ounces) condensed
  cream of mushroom soup
3 soup cans water
1 can (10 fl. ounces) condensed
  turkey noodle soup
1 can (10 fl. ounces) condensed
  vegetarian vegetable soup

Stir mushroom soup until smooth in large saucepan; gradually blend in water. Add remaining soups. Heat thoroughly; stir often. 6 to 8 servings.

CHICKEN CHOWDER

Potatoes and chicken in a creamy blend, farm choice.

½ cup chopped celery
1 tablespoon butter or margarine
1 can (10 fl. ounces) condensed
    cream of potato soup
1 soup can milk
1 can (6 ounces) boned chicken or
    turkey, cut up
1 tablespoon chopped parsley

In saucepan, cook celery in butter until tender. Add remaining ingredients. Heat; stir now and then. 2 to 3 servings.

GUMBO

New Orleans soup with shrimp and ham.

½ cup diced cooked ham
¼ cup chopped celery with leaves
¼ cup chopped green pepper
¼ cup chopped onion
Generous dash leaf thyme
2 tablespoons butter or margarine
2 cans (10 fl. ounces each)
    condensed chicken gumbo soup
2 soup cans water
1 cup cooked shrimp (about ½
    pound uncooked)

Cook ham, celery, green pepper, onion, and thyme in butter until vegetables are tender and ham is browned. Add remaining ingredients. Cook over low heat a few minutes; stir now and then. 4 to 6 servings.

GREEK LEMON SOUP

"Soup Avgolemono" to the Greeks, this has rare delicate tang.

1 can (10 fl. ounces) condensed
    chicken with rice soup
1 soup can water
1 egg
2 teaspoons lemon juice
Nutmeg
Butter

Blend soup and water; heat. Meanwhile, beat egg and lemon juice together in small bowl until well blended. Add a little hot soup to egg mixture; stir constantly. Remove remaining soup from heat; slowly stir in egg mixture (this method prevents curdling). Serve immediately. Garnish with nutmeg or butter, if desired. 2 to 3 servings.

MARDI GRAS GUMBO

Okra, crab, and rice in a flavourful base, gay as the Mardi Gras!

1 can (10 fl. ounces) condensed chicken gumbo soup

1 can (10 fl. ounces) condensed tomato soup

1½ soup cans water

1 can (7 ounces) crab, flaked

2 tablespoons sherry (optional)

2 cups cooked rice

Combine ingredients, except rice. Heat; stir now and then. To serve, line a large bowl or tureen with the cooked rice and pour in. the soup. 4 to 6 servings.

UPPER CANADA PUMPKIN SOUP

Pumpkin purée blends with creamy chicken.

¼ cup finely chopped onion

2 tablespoons butter or margarine

1 can (10 fl. ounces) condensed cream of chicken or mushroom soup

1 cup canned or mashed cooked pumpkin

1 soup can milk

Generous dash ground nutmeg

Dash pepper

In saucepan, cook onion in butter until tender. Add remaining ingredients. Heat; stir now and then. Garnish with parsley. 2 to 3 servings.

POLISH CABBAGE SOUP

A Balkan stew-soup to make a supper.

¾ pound lean pork, cut in small pieces

1 tablespoon butter or margarine

1 can (10 fl. ounces) condensed beef broth

1 can (10 fl. ounces) condensed tomato soup

2 soup cans water

4 cups shredded cabbage (about 1 pound)

½ cup chopped onion

2 teaspoons salt

½ teaspoon paprika

1 bay leaf

Dash pepper

1 tablespoon sherry (optional)

Sour cream

Brown pork in butter. Add remaining ingredients except sour cream. Cover; cook over low heat 30 minutes; stir often. Serve with spoonsful of sour cream. 6 servings.

164

COCK-A-LEEKIE

Scottish wives simmer chicken with leeks and vegetables, serve soup one day, chicken the next. The prunes—a tasty tradition.

2 leeks, thinly sliced
2 tablespoons butter or margarine
2 cans (10 fl. ounces each) condensed chicken vegetable soup
2 soup cans water
4 to 6 cooked prunes (pitted), if desired
½ teaspoon salt
Dash pepper

Cook leeks in butter until tender. Add remaining ingredients. Heat; stir now and then. 4 to 6 servings.

GOULASH SOUP

1 cup cubed cooked beef
¼ cup chopped green pepper
½ teaspoon paprika
2 tablespoons butter or margarine
1 can (10 fl. ounces) condensed tomato soup
1 soup can water
½ teaspoon caraway seed

In saucepan, brown beef and cook green pepper and paprika in butter until green pepper is tender. Add remaining ingredients. Heat; stir now and then. 3 servings.

GREEN AND YELLOW SOUP

⅓ cup shredded cabbage
⅓ cup grated carrot
¼ cup chopped onion
2 tablespoons butter or margarine
1 can (10 fl. ounces) condensed green pea soup
1 soup can water

In saucepan, cook cabbage, carrot, and onion in butter until tender. Add soup and water. Heat; stir now and then. 2 to 3 servings.

POTAGE ST. GERMAIN

This tangy pea soup with chicken is justly famed in France.

1 can (10 fl. ounces) condensed cream of chicken soup
1 can (10 fl. ounces) condensed green pea soup
2 cups milk
½ cup heavy cream
½ cup cooked sliced carrot

Stir soups, milk, and cream until smooth. Add carrot. Heat; stir often. 4 to 6 servings.

PURÉE MONGOLE

A purée is sieved—but you need no strainer for this combination.

1 can (10 fl. ounces) condensed green pea soup
1 can (10 fl. ounces) condensed tomato soup
1 cup milk
1 cup water

Blend soups, milk, and water in saucepan. Heat; stir. Add a dash of curry powder, if desired. 4 servings.

CHINESE SWEET AND SOUR SOUP

Tender chicken pieces in broth with Oriental seasoning.

1 raw chicken breast (½ pound)
¼ teaspoon salt
1 tablespoon cornstarch
3 tablespoons water
1 tablespoon soy sauce
2 cans (10 fl. ounces each) condensed beef broth
1 soup can water
½ cup canned sliced mushrooms and liquid
2 tablespoons vinegar
1 tablespoon sugar
Lemon slices

Skin chicken with sharp knife; cut into thin 2-inch long slices. Sprinkle with salt. Mix cornstarch with 3 tablespoons water and soy sauce; combine with beef broth and water. Bring to boil; stir often; add chicken, mushroom and liquid, vinegar, and sugar. Heat. Simmer 5 minutes. Serve with a slice of lemon in each bowl, a cruet of vinegar on the table. 4 to 6 servings.

MEXICAN FOAM SOUP

¼ cup chopped onion
2 tablespoons chopped green pepper
1 tablespoon butter or margarine
1 can (10 fl. ounces) condensed tomato soup
1 soup can milk
Generous dash red pepper
1 egg, separated

Cook onion and green pepper in butter until tender. Stir in soup, milk, and red pepper. Heat; *but do not boil*. Slightly beat egg yolk; stir a little hot soup into yolk; gradually add to soup. Beat egg white until very soft peaks form; add ½ cup soup mixture; beat lightly. Pour on top of soup; heat. 2 to 3 servings.

BORSCH

There is rare colour and flavour in the bright Russian peasant soup.

2 cups shredded fresh beets
1 tablespoon butter or margarine
1 tablespoon vinegar or lemon juice
2 cans (10 fl. ounces each) condensed consommé
1 can (10 fl. ounces) condensed onion soup
1 soup can water
½ cup tomato juice
2 cups shredded cabbage
¼ to ½ cup sour cream

Cook beets in butter a few minutes. Add vinegar. Cover. Cook over very low heat 20 minutes. Add soups, water, tomato juice, and cabbage. Cover. Cook 10 minutes more or until vegetables are tender. Serve with sour cream (as a garnish or stirred in just before serving). May also be served cold. 5 to 6 servings.

NOTE: If desired, 1 can (14 ounces) beets may be used in place of fresh beets. Chop beets; cook in butter a few minutes. Add remaining ingredients (using liquid from beets plus water, to make 1 cup, in place of water in above recipe). Cover and simmer 10 minutes. Serve with sour cream.

FRENCH ONION SOUP

1 can (10 fl. ounces) condensed onion soup
1 soup can water
2 or 3 slices French or Italian bread (about ½-inch thick)
Butter
Grated Parmesan cheese

Combine soup and water. Heat; let simmer a few minutes. Meanwhile, arrange bread on cookie sheet; spread with butter and sprinkle with Parmesan cheese. Broil until lightly browned. Pour soup into bowls; top each with a cheese croûton. 2 to 3 servings.

GREEN PEA FRANÇAIS

In 17th Century France, peas were the food of kings . . . kingly still.

¼ cup canned mushroom stems and pieces
1 tablespoon butter or margarine
2 cans (10 fl. ounces each) condensed green pea soup
2 soup cans water and mushroom liquid
1 cup grated carrot

Drain mushrooms, saving liquid. Sauté in butter. Add soup, water, and mushroom liquid; stir until smooth. Add carrot. Heat; simmer 10 minutes or until carrot is tender and flavours blended. 4 to 6 servings.

167

SENEGALESE SOUP

Curry and chicken have an affinity in the soup bowl, too.

1 can (10 fl. ounces) condensed
  cream of chicken soup
⅛ teaspoon curry powder
1 soup can milk

Stir soup; blend in curry powder. Add milk gradually. Place in refrigerator for at least 4 hours. Serve in chilled bowls. 2 to 3 servings.

VATAPA

Unusual South American blend of broth, shellfish, nuts.

1 can (10 fl. ounces) condensed
  beef broth
2 cans (10 fl. ounces each) condensed clam chowder Manhattan
  style
2 soup cans water
½ cup chopped salted peanuts
¼ cup flaked coconut
1 bay leaf
Few drops "Tabasco" sauce
1 pound shrimp, peeled and
  deveined

Combine all ingredients except shrimp; cover and bring to boil; stir often. Add shrimp; simmer 5 minutes or until tender. Remove bay leaf before serving. 8 servings.

LOBSTER CHOWDER

¼ cup chopped onion
2 tablespoons butter or margarine
2 cans (10 fl. ounces each)
  condensed Cheddar cheese soup
1 soup can milk
1 soup can water
1 cup flaked cooked lobster
2 tablespoons chopped parsley
Dash pepper
Dash paprika

Cook onion in butter until tender. Stir in soup until smooth; gradually blend in milk and water. Add lobster, parsley, and pepper. Heat; stir often. Garnish with paprika. 4 to 6 servings.

TURKEY VEGETABLE CUP

¼ cup canned mushroom stems
  and pieces, drained
1 tablespoon butter or margarine
Dash leaf thyme, crushed
1 can (10 fl. ounces) condensed
  turkey vegetable soup
1 soup can water

Brown mushrooms in butter with thyme. Stir in soup and water. Heat. 2 to 3 servings.

VARIATION: Substitute ¼ cup diced chopped ham for mushrooms and dash ground marjoram for thyme, if desired.

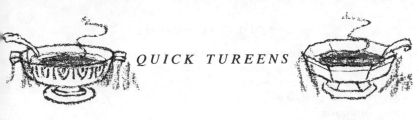

A new group of great soups takes high honours these days. Subtle flavour-blends challenge the great soups of the past. These are quickly created by combining canned soups in generous proportions and adding accents of other foods for tantilizing flavour.

MARITIME FISH SOUP

½ cup chopped onion
1 tablespoon butter or margarine
1 can (10 fl. ounces) condensed cream of celery soup
1 can (10 fl. ounces) condensed clam chowder Manhattan style
1½ soup cans water
1 cup flaked cooked white fish or tuna (7-ounce can, drained and flaked) or shrimp (4¼-ounce can, drained)
1 tablespoon chopped parsley

Cook onion in butter until tender. Blend in remaining ingredients. Simmer a few minutes; stir often. 6 servings.

BEANSTRONI

1 cup diced cooked ham
2 tablespoons chopped onion
1 tablespoon butter or margarine
1 can (10 fl. ounces) bean with bacon soup
2 soup cans water
1 can (10 fl. ounces) condensed minestrone soup

Brown ham and onion in butter. Stir in bean with bacon soup; blend in water. Add minestrone soup. Heat; stir often. 4 to 6 servings.

MEATBALL SOUP

½ pound ground beef, seasoned
1 can (10 fl. ounces) condensed bean with bacon, celery, mushroom, green pea, minestrone, onion, tomato, or vegetable soup
1 soup can water

Shape meat into 20 small meatballs; brown slowly in saucepan. (Use a little shortening if necessary.) Pour off any excess drippings. Stir in soup and water; simmer a few minutes. 2 to 3 servings.

169

SPRING SOUP BOWL

2 tablespoons chopped onion
1 tablespoon butter or margarine
1 can (10 fl. ounces) condensed French Canadian style pea soup
1 soup can water
2 tablespoons chopped pimiento

Cook onion in butter until tender. Add soup; gradually stir in water. Add pimiento. Heat; stir often. 2 to 3 servings.

COUNTRY FAVOURITE

2 slices bacon
2 tablespoons chopped onion
Dash leaf thyme, crushed
1 can (10 fl. ounces) condensed beef noodle soup
1 soup can water
½ cup cooked cut green beans

Cook bacon until crisp; remove and crumble. Pour off all but 1 table-spoon drippings. Add onion and thyme; cook until onion is tender. Add soup, water, and beans. Heat; stir often. Top each serving with bacon. 3 servings.

VEGETABLE WIENER SOUP

1 wiener, thinly sliced
2 tablespoons chopped onion
1 tablespoon butter or margarine
1 can (10 fl. ounces) condensed old fashioned vegetable soup
1 soup can water

Brown wiener slices and onion in butter. Stir in soup and water. Heat; stir often. 2 to 3 servings.

CANADIAN COUNTRY SOUP

4 ounces sliced back bacon, cut into small pieces
½ cup chopped onion
1 tablespoon butter or margarine
1 can (10 fl. ounces) condensed bean with bacon soup
1 can (10 fl. ounces) condensed cream of mushroom soup
1 can (10 fl. ounces) condensed vegetarian vegetable soup
2 soup cans water
1 cup drained cooked whole kernel corn

Brown bacon and cook onion in butter until tender. Blend in soups and water; add corn. Heat; stir often. 6 to 8 servings.

170

Upper Canada Pumpkin Soup Page 164

HEARTY BEEF SOUP

2 ounces sliced dried beef,
   cut into small pieces
¼ cup chopped onion
2 tablespoons butter or margarine
1 can (10 fl. ounces) condensed
   cream of celery soup
1 can (10 fl. ounces) condensed
   cream of mushroom soup
1 soup can water
½ soup can milk
1 cup cooked corn
½ cup cooked tomatoes

Pour boiling water over beef; drain. In saucepan, cook beef and onion in butter until onion is tender. Add soups; stir until smooth. Add remaining ingredients. Heat; stir often. 4 servings.

CRAB BISQUE

¼ cup chopped onion
⅛ teaspoon leaf thyme
1 tablespoon butter or margarine
1 can (10 fl. ounces) condensed
   Cheddar cheese soup
½ soup can milk
½ soup can water
1 cup flaked cooked crab (or
   5-ounce can, drained)
¼ cup chopped cooked broccoli
Lemon wedges

Cook onion and thyme in butter until onion is tender. Add remaining ingredients except lemon wedges. Heat; stir often. Serve with lemon wedges. 3 servings.

CELERY TURKEY TUREEN

¼ cup chopped onion
1 tablespoon butter or margarine
1 can (10 fl. ounces) condensed
   cream of celery soup
1 can (10 fl. ounces) condensed
   turkey noodle soup
1 cup milk
1 cup water
1 cup cream-style corn
Chopped parsley

Cook onion slowly in butter until tender but not browned. Blend in soups, milk, and water, add corn. Heat; stir often. Serve with a garnish of chopped parsley. 4 to 6 servings.

CHICKEN MUSHROOM POTAGE

1 can (10 fl. ounces) condensed
   cream of mushroom soup
1 can (10 fl. ounces) condensed
   chicken vegetable soup
1½ soup cans water
1 cup chopped fresh spinach
1 cup diced cooked ham

Stir cream of mushroom soup until smooth. Add remaining ingredients. Heat; stir often. 4 to 6 servings. Garnish with dash of mace.

CHICKEN CANJA

½ cup diced cooked ham
1 tablespoon butter or margarine
1 can (10 fl. ounces) condensed
   cream of chicken soup
1 can (10 fl. ounces) condensed
   chicken vegetable soup
2 soup cans water
1 tablespoon chopped parsley

Lightly brown ham in butter. Blend in soups, water, and parsley. Heat; stir often. 4 to 6 servings.

SHRIMP-POTATO SOUP

2 cans (10 fl. ounces each)
   condensed cream of potato soup
2 soup cans milk
1 cup diced cooked shrimp
½ cup cooked whole kernel corn
¼ cup chopped parsley
Generous dash hot pepper sauce

In saucepan, combine all ingredients. Heat; stir now and then. 4 to 6 servings.

TUNA VEGETABLE BOWL

2 tablespoons chopped onion
2 tablespoons chopped parsley
Dash leaf thyme
2 tablespoons butter or margarine
1 can (10 fl. ounces) condensed
   cream of celery soup
1 can (10 fl. ounces) condensed
   vegetarian vegetable soup
2 soup cans water
1 can (7 ounces) tuna, drained
   and flaked

Cook onion, parsley, and thyme in butter until onion is tender. Blend in soups, and water. Add tuna. Heat; stir often. 4 to 6 servings.

Frosty Soups

Count three special appeals for cold summer soups. They are taste-tantalizing appetizers, as in creamy smooth Vichyssoise, or shimmering jellied consommé. They make refreshing pickups to sip when you want to feel cooler. They look inviting, set out on the table in ice-lined bowls, or garnished with fresh vegetables.

Cold soups were made fashionable back in the seventeenth century by Louis XIV—for a very practical reason. Each of the king's dishes was tasted by several people before it came to him. The monarch grew tired of lukewarm soup, and requested tasty cold soups, instead.

EASY CHILLED SOUPS

The following condensed soups are excellent to serve cold.

To prepare, mix soup with water or milk as desired. Chill about 4 hours. For quicker service, keep cans of soup in refrigerator; then blend with cold water or milk at meal-time.

Bisque of Tomato
Consommé (Chill to jell; do not add liquid)
Cream of Asparagus
Cream of Celery
Cream of Chicken
Cream of Potato
Green Pea
Tomato

AVOCADO CHICKEN BOWL

1 can (10 fl. ounces) condensed cream of chicken soup
1 soup can milk
½ cup chopped celery
1 to 2 tablespoons chopped onion
1 ripe avocado, mashed

In blender, combine all ingredients except avocado; blend until smooth. Chill at least 4 hours. Add avocado; blend until smooth. Thin to desired consistency with milk. Serve immediately in chilled bowls. 2 to 3 servings.

AUTUMN FROST

1 can (10 fl. ounces) condensed
  bisque of tomato soup
1 can (10 fl. ounces) condensed
  consommé
1 soup can water
1 to 2 teaspoons sherry (optional)
Lemon slices

Combine soups, water, and sherry. Heat; stir now and then. Chill 4 hours. Serve in icy cold bowls. Garnish each serving with a lemon slice. 4 servings.

CRAB BOWL

1 can (10 fl. ounces) condensed
  cream of celery soup
1 soup can water
½ cup flaked cooked crab
1 tablespoon thinly sliced green
  onion
½ medium tomato, cut in cubes
¼ teaspoon grated lemon rind
Lemon wedges

Blend soup and water; stir in crab, onion, tomato, and lemon rind. Place in refrigerator for at least 4 hours. Serve in chilled bowls; garnish with lemon wedges. 2 to 3 servings.

DUTCH POTAGE

1 cup shredded cabbage
¼ cup shredded carrot
¼ teaspoon caraway seed
1 tablespoon butter or margarine
1 can (10 fl. ounces) condensed
  cream of potato soup
1 cup milk
½ cup sour cream

In saucepan, cook cabbage and carrot with caraway in butter until tender. Add remaining ingredients. Heat; stir now and then. Chill 4 hours or more. Thin to desired consistency. Serve in chilled bowls. 2 to 3 servings.

CUCUMBER COOLER

1 can (10 fl. ounces) condensed
  cream of celery soup
1 cup milk
1 small cucumber, diced (about 1
  cup)
Dash "Tabasco" sauce
Dash salt and pepper
1 cup sour cream

Combine soup, milk, cucumber, "Tabasco" sauce, and seasonings in electric blender; blend for 2 minutes. Stir in sour cream. Place in refrigerator for at least 4 hours. Serve in chilled bowls. 3 to 4 servings.

JELLIED SOUP-SALAD

2 cans (10 fl. ounces each)
  condensed consommé
¼ cup diced green pepper
2 tablespoons chopped parsley
1 tablespoon minced onion
1 tablespoon butter or margarine
½ teaspoon curry powder
¼ cup slivered blanched almonds
Dash salt

Combine consommé, green pepper, parsley, and onion. Chill until jellied—about 4 hours. Stir when partially jellied to distribute vegetables. Melt butter in a small frying pan; add curry powder, almonds, and salt. Cook over low heat, until lightly browned; drain. Serve consommé in chilled bowls; top with almonds. 4 servings.

LOBSTER POT

2 cans (10 fl. ounces each)
  condensed consommé
1 can (5 ounces) lobster, drained
  and flaked
½ cup cubed avocado
¼ cup chopped celery
2 tablespoons chopped green onion
2 tablespoons lemon juice
Dash "Tabasco" sauce
Dash pepper

Combine consommé with other ingredients. Chill until jellied—about 4 hours. Stir when partially jellied to distribute lobster and vegetables. Serve with lemon wedges, if desired. 4 to 6 servings.

GAZPACHO

1 can (10 fl. ounces) condensed
  tomato soup
1 cup water
1 tablespoon olive oil
2 tablespoons wine vinegar
1 large clove garlic, minced
1 cup finely chopped cucumber
½ cup finely chopped green pepper
¼ cup finely chopped onion

In bowl, combine soup, water, oil, vinegar, and garlic. Chill 4 hours. Serve in chilled bowls. Pass chilled vegetables for garnishes (also croûtons if desired). 3 servings.

PARFAIT CONSOMMÉ

1 can (10 fl. ounces) condensed
  consommé
½ cup sour cream
2 tablespoons chopped chives

Place unopened can of consommé in refrigerator until jellied, about 4 hours. To serve, spoon a little consommé into each parfait glass; top with sour cream. Repeat layers; sprinkle chives on top. 2 to 3 servings.

SOUP-ON-THE-ROCKS

The easiest and most popular of frosted soups is yours to enjoy anywhere. Simply fill a broad glass with ice cubes. Pour beef broth, right from the can, over the cubes. Garnish with a slice or wedge of lemon or lime. NOTE: For variety add a fleck of spice to the beef broth before pouring over ice cubes, perhaps curry, nutmeg, cinnamon, allspice, or ginger.

CREAMY MOUNTAIN REFRESHER

1　can (10 fl. ounces) condensed cream of potato soup
1　soup can milk
½　cup sour cream
¼　cup finely chopped cucumber

In saucepan, combine all ingredients. Heat; stir now and then. Beat until smooth with blender; or use rotary beater or electric mixer and strain. Chill 4 hours or more. Thin to desired consistency. Serve in chilled bowls. 3 servings.

SHRIMP GLACÉ

1　can (10 fl. ounces) condensed cream of celery soup
1　soup can water
1　cup diced cooked shrimp
1　cup chopped fresh spinach
¼　cup chopped celery
½　teaspoon grated lemon rind

In saucepan, combine all ingredients. Heat; stir now and then. Chill 4 hours or more. Serve in chilled bowls. 3 servings.
GARNISHES: Top with choice of chopped watercress, stuffed olive slices, minced parsley, snipped chives, radish slices, or slivered toasted almonds.

Twentieth-century chef Louis Diat invented one of the most famous frosty soups, Vichyssoise, at the Ritz-Carlton in New York City—and what a success it was! Now you can try Vichyssoise in at least four quick versions, or add your own to this chapter of cold summer soups.

VICHYSSOISE

1 can (10 fl. ounces) condensed
　cream of potato soup
1 soup can milk
Chopped chives or parsley

In saucepan, combine soup and milk. Heat; stir now and then. Beat until smooth with blender; or use rotary beater or electric mixer and strain. Chill 4 hours or more. Thin to desired consistency. Serve in chilled bowls. Garnish with chives or parsley. 2 to 3 servings.

FLORENTINE VICHYSSOISE

1 can (10 fl. ounces) condensed
　cream of potato soup
1 soup can milk
¼ cup cooked chopped spinach
Nutmeg

In saucepan, combine all ingredients except nutmeg. Heat; stir now and then. Beat until smooth with blender; or use rotary beater or electric mixer and strain. Chill 4 hours or more. Thin to desired consistency. Serve in chilled bowls. Garnish with nutmeg. 2 to 3 servings.

PINK VICHYSSOISE

1 can (10 fl. ounces) condensed
　cream of potato soup
¾ cup milk
½ cup tomato juice
Dash garlic powder
¼ cup chopped green pepper

In saucepan, combine soup, milk, tomato juice, and garlic. Heat; stir now and then. Beat until smooth with blender; or use rotary beater or electric mixer and strain. Chill 4 hours or more. Thin to desired consistency. Add green pepper. Serve in chilled bowls. 2 to 3 servings.

Dress-Up Garnishes

"Only the pure in heart can make a good soup" Beethoven wrote. The artistic can dress it up, he might have added. When soup comes to the table—hot or cold, thick or clear—a bit of contrast in texture, colour, or flavour sets it off to appetizing advantage.

Achieve soup distinctiveness through garnishes such as these which are good on most any soup: chopped parsley, watercress, or chives— thin-sliced lemon or grated rind—sliced cooked mushrooms—sour cream or salted whipped cream—packaged stuffing—toasted nuts—sliced green onions—chopped ripe olives—crisp bacon—potato chips and corn chips —crisp cereal.

Many recipes follow for other ideas.

ZESTY PAN-TOASTED CRACKERS

1 cup oyster crackers
1 tablespoon butter, melted
Celery or onion salt

Add crackers to butter; heat. Shake pan to coat crackers with butter. Sprinkle with celery or onion salt. Especially good with tomato or chicken soup.

CHEESE CHOICE

Cheese adds a tangy accent to soups. Worth trying; shredded Swiss cheese on old fashioned tomato rice soup. Grated Parmesan cheese on minestrone soup. Shredded sharp yellow cheese sprinkled on jellied consommé. Snippets (shapes cut from thin-sliced cheese) floated on top of soup (good on most kinds).

SOUR CREAM TOPPING

Try a dollop of sour cream atop soup—hot or cold. Good alone or combined with horseradish or watercress. Add parsley or chopped peeled cucumber for chilled cream of celery, chicken, mushroom soup or jellied consommé. Combine sour cream and chives to top beef broth, tomato, jellied consommé, or beef with vegetables and barley soup.

WHIPPED CREAM GARNISHES

Combine ¼ cup heavy cream (whipped) with ½ teaspoon prepared horseradish; spoon on green pea soup. Or to ¼ cup heavy cream (whipped) add 1 teaspoon grated lime rind, ½ teaspoon sherry (optional) for jellied consommé. Or try ¼ teaspoon minced onion in cream for beef broth-tomato soup.

EASY DUMPLINGS

¼ cup packaged biscuit mix
4 teaspoons milk

Lightly blend biscuit mix and milk. Drop small amounts of dough from tip of a teaspoon into simmering chunky turkey or condensed vegetable beef soup. Cook for 5 minutes; cover and cook another 5 minutes.

VARIATIONS: 1. Season biscuit mix with 1 teaspoon minced parsley. Cook in chicken vegetable soup. 2. Add ¼ cup shredded sharp Canadian Cheddar cheese to biscuit mix; blend with milk. Cook in vegetarian vegetable soup. 3. Sprinkle dumplings with Parmesan cheese. Cook in minestrone soup. 4. Add 1 tablespoon chopped watercress or 1 teaspoon minced onion to biscuit mix; cook in turkey noodle soup.

CURRIED CRAX

⅛ teaspoon curry powder
1 tablespoon butter, melted
½ cup wheat squares or coarsely
    crumbled saltines

Stir curry powder into butter. Add crackers; heat to brown lightly. Stir often. TIP: Substitute ⅛ teaspoon leaf thyme for curry. Proceed as above. Good on most chicken soups or cream of potato soup.

ONION TIDBITS

¼ teaspoon instant minced onion
1 tablespoon butter, melted
½ cup cheese tidbits

Stir minced onion into butter. Add cheese tidbits; heat to brown lightly. Stir often. Serve on tomato or cream of chicken soup.

SOUP ACCENTS

Almond-Orange: Sprinkle chopped toasted almonds and grated orange rind on heated cream of asparagus or chicken soup.

Diced tomato: Float on jellied consommé.

Thin sliced onion: Float on top of shimmering jellied consommé.

Chopped celery: Sprinkle on consommé.

Chopped or thinly sliced pickle: Sprinkle on old fashioned tomato rice soup.

Popcorn: Sprinkle on any soup.

Pretzels: Sprinkle on hearty or thick soups.

CROÛTON CREATIONS

Crisp croûtons dress up soup easily, can be flavoured "to your taste" quickly.

BASIC DIRECTIONS

1 slice white bread, cut into cubes,
2 tablespoons butter or margarine, melted

In frying pan, brown bread cubes in butter; stir constantly. Season to set off soup flavour.

BASIL OR OREGANO

Sprinkle croûtons with ¼ teaspoon sweet basil or ground oregano. Serve with tomato or minestrone soup.

PARMESAN CHEESE

Sprinkle croûtons with 1 tablespoon grated Parmesan cheese. Add to green pea or minestrone soup.

CURRY

Sprinkle croûtons with curry powder. Add to chicken with rice or cream of chicken or green pea soup.

GARLIC

Melt butter in frying pan; add ½ small clove garlic, minced. Lightly mix in bread cubes; cook over low heat, stirring constantly, until bread is crisp and brown. Serve on vegetable or green pea, beef with vegetables and barley or beef noodle soup.

SAGE OR THYME

Add dash of ground sage or leaf thyme to croûtons. Serve with chicken with rice or vegetable soup.

Soup Servers' Almanac

FALL

Brisk winds mark the end of summer. Drive to the country for a pie squash and basket of apples. Pack a vacuum of CLOVE-SEASONED BEEF TOMATO JUG: Combine 1 can each (10 fl. ounces) condensed beef broth and condensed tomato soup. Stir in 1½ soup cans water, 1 teaspoon lemon juice, dash ground cloves. Simmer a few minutes; pour into vacuum jug and sip (for 4) at a roadside stop.

Leaves changing colour in the woods. Follow an autumnal walk with a warming mug of RUSSET SOUP: Combine 1 can (10 fl. ounces) condensed old fashioned vegetable soup, ½ soup can tomato juice, ½ soup can water. Heat and serve to 2 or 3.

Or try ROSY ONION SOUP: 1 can (10 fl. ounces) condensed onion soup, ½ soup can tomato juice, ½ soup can water. Combine and heat to serve 2 or 3 autumn gardeners.

Early frost. Cover delicate garden plants. Dress children in warm jackets for back-to-school; fix warm lunches, too. HEARTY HAM GUMBO: Brown ¼ cup diced cooked ham in 1 tablespoon butter or margarine. Add 1 can (10 fl. ounces) condensed chicken gumbo soup, 1 soup can water, dash "Tabasco" sauce. Heat to serve 2 or 3.

Add extra vitamins to lunch for your young scholars. VEGETABLE TURKEY NOODLE: Combine 1 can (10 fl. ounces) condensed turkey noodle soup, 1 can water. Add ¼ cup diced cooked carrots, 1 tablespoon chopped parsley. Heat to make 3 mugs.

Football weather crisp and clear. Pack a blanket and a vacuum bottle of soup. TOUCHDOWN SPECIAL: Combine 1 can (10 fl. ounces) condensed green pea soup, 1 soup can water, generous dash leaf thyme. Heat, stir often, and pour into small vacuum holding 3 cups; 2 to 3 servings. Double this for extra servings.

CHICKEN RICE CONFETTI is a warmer, too: Combine 1 can (10 fl. ounces) condensed chicken with rice soup, 1 soup can water, 1 teaspoon finely chopped parsley, 1 teaspoon finely chopped pimiento. Heat; stir often. For 2 or 3.

Late Indian summer with excellent vacation weather. Refresh on arrival with GARDEN TOMATO SOUP: Cook 2 tablespoons chopped green pepper, 2 tablespoons chopped onion, dash oregano in 2 tablespoons butter or margarine until vegetables are tender. Add 1 can (10 fl. ounces) condensed old fashioned tomato rice soup, 1 soup can water. Heat; stir often. Serve to 2 or 3.

Thanksgiving. Begin dinner with a traditional soup . . . onion or cream of mushroom. Or try this unique GREEN PEPPER CREAM: In blender, combine 1 can (10 fl. ounces) condensed cream of celery soup, 1 soup can milk, 3 tablespoons chopped green pepper, and 1 tablespoon chopped onion. Cover; blend until smooth. Pour into saucepan. Heat; stir now and then. 2 to 3 servings. Multiply recipe according to guests you expect.

POST-THANKSGIVING TURKEY SOUP: Cook 1 small chopped onion in 2 tablespoons butter or margarine. Add 1 can (10 fl. ounces) condensed chicken vegetable soup and blend with 2 soup cans water; add 1 can (10 fl. ounces) condensed turkey noodle soup, 1 cup diced cooked turkey, and 1 tablespoon chopped parsley. Heat. Stir often. 4 servings.

Northeasters blowing late October and start of November. Snug time for home parties. Ward off winds outside with warm CHICKEN-ALMOND CURRY SOUP: In saucepan, cook ¼ cup slivered almonds, 2 tablespoons chopped onion, ½ teaspoon curry powder in 1 tablespoon butter or margarine until almonds are lightly browned. Blend in 1 can each (10 fl. ounces) condensed cream of chicken soup and chicken with rice soup. Add 1½ soup cans water. Heat for 4 to 6 servings.

Sadie Hawkins Day. Plan a supper soup to please a man. CARAWAY BACON BOWL: Cook 2 ounces back bacon (cut in strips), ¼ cup chopped onion, ¼ teaspoon caraway seed, until onion is tender. Add 1 can (10 fl. ounces) condensed cream of celery soup, 1 soup can water, 1 cup shredded cabbage. Bring to boil. Cover; simmer 10 minutes or until cabbage is tender. Serves a hearty-eating couple.

For a party, try TRIPLE PLAY SOUPS: Blend 1 can each (10 fl. ounces) condensed beef noodle, bean with bacon and cream of celery soup, 2 soup cans water. Add 2 tablespoons chopped parsley, 1 tablespoon Worcestershire; heat and serve to 6 or 8.

WINTER

Christmas Eve. Traditional in many homes is an oyster stew supper. Use the soup just as it is . . . or garnish with wedges of ripe olive or golden shreds of carrot or cheese. Finish the feast with a fruit bowl (shiny red apples and bright tangerines); Christmas cookies; coffee or tea.

When carolers fill the air with Christmas spirit thank them with TOMATO SOUP PUNCH: Combine 1 can (10 fl. ounces) condensed tomato soup, 1 soup can milk, ⅛ teaspoon ground cinnamon, dash ground cloves. Beat with a rotary beater. Simmer a few minutes. Garnish each serving with whipped cream. Makes 4 to 5 punch cups.

Sleigh-riding weather frequent between Christmas and New Year's.
Warm winter sports fans with soups that make the most of the last of your
holiday ham. Three ways (count them) to make a little ham go far for
family meals:

---

1. OYSTER HAM STEW: Combine 1 can (10 fl. ounces) condensed
oyster stew with 1 soup can milk, 1 cup cubed cooked potatoes, ½ cup
diced cooked ham, 1 tablespoon chopped parsley, ⅛ teaspoon leaf thyme.
Heat; stir now and then. 2 to 3 servings.

---

2. HAM CREAM BOWL: Brown ½ cup diced cooked ham in 1 tablespoon butter or margarine. Add 1 can each (10 fl. ounces) condensed
cream of celery and chicken vegetable soup, 2 soup cans water, 1 tablespoon chopped parsley, pinch crushed rosemary leaves. Heat; stir often. 4
to 6 servings.

---

3. HAM FINALE: Combine 1 can (10 fl. ounces) condensed chicken
noodle soup, 1 soup can water, ¼ cup diced cooked ham, 1 tablespoon
chopped green pepper. Simmer until pepper is tender-crisp; stir. 2 to 3
servings.

Chinese New Year. Between January 21 and February 12, the Chinese
Kitchen God is sent to heaven to report the doings of the household. Be
sure he makes a good report on goings-on at your house.
Serve an easy CHINESE SOUP: Combine 1 can (10 fl. ounces) condensed beef broth, 1 soup can water, 2 teaspoons soy sauce. Heat to boiling. Add ¼ cup diced carrots, ¼ cup chopped green beans. Cover; simmer 15 minutes or until vegetables are tender. Serves 2 to 3.

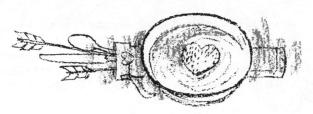

February is long on snow, rain, and holidays. Holiday lunches are easy with
LAURENTIAN GUMBO: Combine 1 can (10 fl. ounces) condensed
chicken gumbo soup, 1 soup can water, ¼ cup cooked crab, fish, or shrimp.
Heat; stir now and then. 2 to 3 servings.

VALENTINE CROÛTON SOUP: Drain and cook ¼ cup canned
mushroom stems and pieces with 1 tablespoon chopped parsley in 1 tablespoon butter or margarine until mushrooms are lightly browned. Add 1 can
(10 fl. ounces) condensed chicken noodle soup, 1 soup can water, 1 tablespoon sherry (optional). Heat; stir. Cut small hearts out of bread slices,
brown lightly in butter. Top each serving with heart croûton. Serve to your
love and you.

Or simply serve the heart croûtons on rosy red Tomato Soup.

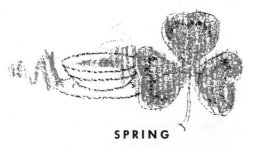

SPRING

March windy and sunny. Time to order seeds. St. Patrick's Day and
green is on the menu. For a simple celebration, just heat a can of cream of
potato soup as directed. Garnish with parsley or watercress. Or you might
serve green pea soup . . . topped with a fluff of unsweetened whipped cream.

SPRING GREEN SOUP tastes like a party. Cook ¼ cup chopped onion
in 1 tablespoon butter or margarine until tender. Stir in 1 can (10 fl.
ounces) condensed cream of celery soup, 1½ soup cans milk; ½ cup
drained chopped cooked spinach, dash sweet basil. Heat; stir often. 3
servings.

187

April showers and Lenten meals call for hearty meatless soups. A quartet of chowders.

GARDEN CHOWDER: Combine 1 can (10 fl. ounces) condensed New England clam chowder, 1 soup can milk, ½ cup cooked carrots (cut in strips), 2 tablespoons chopped parsley. Heat; stir now and then. 2 to 3 servings.

SHRIMP CHOWDER: Cook ¼ cup chopped onion in 2 tablespoons butter or margarine until tender. Blend in 2 cans (10 fl. ounces each) condensed cream of celery or mushroom soup, 1 soup can each of milk and water, 1 cup cooked shrimp (4¼ ounce can, drained), 2 tablespoons chopped parsley, dash pepper. Heat. Garnish each serving with paprika. 6 to 8 servings. TUNA CHOWDER: Repeat the previous recipe, except omit the shrimp and add 1 cup drained flaked tuna (7-ounce can) instead. LOBSTER OR CRAB CHOWDER: You can make the same soup with 1 cup flaked cooked lobster or crab (or 5-ounce can, drained) instead of shrimp or tuna.

For an elegant Lenten soup serve SOUP THYME: Blend 1 can (10 fl. ounces) condensed green pea soup with 1 soup can water and ⅛ teaspoon ground thyme. Heat; stir now and then. Garnish each serving with unsweetened whipped cream or sour cream. Serve to 2 or 3.

Easter Sunday dinner is a family tradition in many homes. Whether the main course is ham or lamb, plan a soup for a perfect prelude . . . perhaps chicken with rice or cream of asparagus.

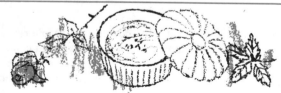

Mother's Day and time to flatter the daily soup maker with a flavourful bowl pretty as a bouquet. MINTED PEA SOUP: Blend 1 can (10 fl. ounces) condensed green pea soup and 1 soup can water. Add ¼ cup thinly sliced carrot, 1 tablespoon sliced green onion and 1 teaspoon crushed dried mint flakes. Heat; stir now and then. Garnish with sour cream for 2 or 3 servings.

188

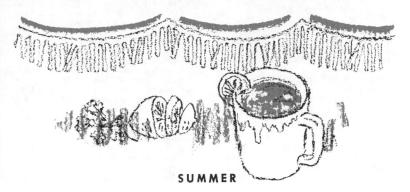

SUMMER

Early warm days relieved by cool soups to sip. TOMATO TANG: Blend 1 can (10 fl. ounces) condensed tomato soup and 1 soup can water. Stir in ½ teaspoon grated lemon rind. Place in refrigerator for at least 4 hours. Serve in chilled bowls; garnish with parsley or lemon slice to refresh 2 or 3.

Beware sudden chill after early-summer swim. Warm up with CONSOMMÉ RISOTTO: Combine 1 can (10 fl. ounces) condensed consommé, 1 soup can water, and ¼ cup cooked rice. Heat; stir often. Serve to 2 or 3.

One hot dish is the old rule for a cold meal. Make yours SAVOURY CONSOMMÉ: Cook ¼ cup chopped green pepper and 1 tablespoon thinly sliced green onion in 2 tablespoons butter or margarine until tender. Add 2 cans (10 fl. ounces each) condensed consommé, 1½ soup cans water and 2 whole cloves. Simmer a few minutes to blend flavours. Remove cloves before serving to 4 or 5.

August sunny; corn ripens. Try kernels in CORN OYSTER STEW: Cook 2 tablespoons small thin green pepper strips and 2 tablespoons chopped green onion in 1 tablespoon butter or margarine until vegetables are tender. Add 1 can (10 fl. ounces) condensed oyster stew, 1 soup can milk and ½ cup cooked whole kernel corn. Heat; stir now and then. 2 to 3 servings.

For small-fry sailors, deck a green pea "sea" of soup with a cracker SAILBOAT: Spread 2 round crackers with peanut butter. Cut 1 saltine in half diagonally so you have two triangles. Stand the half cracker in the peanut butter to make a "sail". Float sailboat on soup. 2 sailboats for *fair weather ahead.*

INDEX

194

195

197

Campbell Soup Company Ltd is the authorized
user of trademarks "Campbell's" and "V-8"